OVER 200 QUESTIONS
CHILDREN ASK ABOUT
FRIENDS, SCHOOL
& OUR WORLD

Over 200 Questions Children Ask about friends school & our world

General Editor:
Daryl J. Lucas

Contributers:
David R. Veerman, M.Div
James C. Galvin, Ed.D.
James C. Wilhoit, Ph.D.
Richard Osborne
Jonathan Farrar

Illustrator:
Lillian Crump

Tyndale House Publishers, Inc., Wheaton, Illinois

Visit Tyndale's exciting Web site at www.tyndale.com

Series designed by Jane Joseph

Over 200 Questions Children Ask about Friends, School & Our World contains material from the following previously published books:

106 Questions Children Ask about Our World and *108 Questions Children Ask about Friends and School,* produced for Tyndale House Publishers by Lightwave Publishing, Inc. and The Livingstone Corporation.

Scripture quotations are taken from the *Holy Bible,* New Living Translation, copyright © 1996. Used by permission of Tyndale House Publishers, Inc., Wheaton, Illinois 60189. All rights reserved.

ISBN 0-8423-8638-6 softcover
ISBN-0-8423-8637-8 hardcover
ISBN 0-8423-8642-4 FCP edition

Printed in the United States of America

05   04   03
5   4   3   2   1

CONTENTS

NOTE FROM THE WRITERS

Every person has an inborn need for relationships—the need to love and be loved. It's no wonder, then, that our children want to have enjoyable and affirming friendships. And the older they get, the more important friends become. As a result, our children will naturally ask about how to make friends, how to be a good friend, and how to navigate the sometimes stormy seas of friendship.

As children get involved in school, these questions about friends will increase, as will, quite naturally, the questions about teachers, homework, classes, the fledgling pressures of academia, and the world in general.

One of those growing pressures is the push for popularity. Actually, this pressure usually results from the issues related to the combination of friends and school. Children want to be accepted and liked, and they enjoy being with the kids who seem to make things happen on campus. Thus, popularity will also engender a multitude of questions, some of them pretty tough.

Easy responses to tough questions are "I don't know!" or "Just because!" or "Because I said so!" These may be responses, but they're not answers. And they certainly don't help the child sort truth from error.

These tough questions are the reason for this book. We collected hundreds of questions children asked about friends and school as well as our changing world. Then we identified over 200 of the most common and important ones and sorted them into categories. If you are a parent of children ages three to ten or if you work with children, you have surely heard questions like these. If not, you soon will.

After identifying Bible passages relevant to each question, we answer the question, summarizing the Bible's application. Study the Scriptures listed, because the Bible has a lot to say about relationships—in the neighborhood and at school. It doesn't answer every question directly, but it gives principles that Christians should know and follow.

As you answer children's questions, keep in mind the following points:

- **"Silly" questions are serious questions.** Always take children's questions seriously. Don't laugh at them. Some questions may sound silly to you, but they're not silly to your child. Be careful not to ridicule your child's imaginative ideas.

- **Some questions reflect a child's immediate personal concerns.** For example, when a little girl asks, "If my friends ignore me, should I ignore them?" (question 33), she's asking about her friends, not just the reaction she should exhibit. She knows that being ignored is not fun and that friends should not ignore other friends. She wants assurance that true friends will not ignore her. Go ahead and answer the "question behind the question": assure your child that true friends do not ignore other friends. If you suspect that there may be a hidden question but don't know what it is, a great way to get at it is to say, "Why do you ask?" or "Why do you want to know?"

- **The best answers come from Scripture.** The Bible doesn't answer every curiosity, but it is the only authoritative source we have for information on how to live in this world. The best thing you can do to prepare to answer questions like these is to study the Scriptures yourself.

- **The best answers avoid theological jargon.** Use normal words. Children think in literal terms, so abstract concepts are meaningless to them. As much as possible, talk about *events* and *objects* that they can imagine. Describe a smell. Mention a specific thing. Talk about an action, such as running. Give them something to look at in their minds. If they can see it, they will understand it.

- **Some questions have no answer.** Be careful not to make up an answer when you don't have one and when the Bible is silent. If you don't have an answer, say so. Or suggest that you look for the answer together. If you get in the habit of inventing answers, your children will later lump faith with stories and superstitions they've discovered are false. Emphasize the truths of Scripture that you *do* know.

- **Some kids just want to keep asking.** Be ready for follow-up questions and be willing to keep talking. Your answer may lead to more questions. That's the mark of a good answer—it makes the child think.

We wrote this book to help you answer kids' questions about friends, school, and our world. We sincerely hope and pray it does that.

—Dave Veerman, Jim Galvin, Jim Wilhoit, Daryl Lucas, Rick Osborne, Jon Farrar, Lillian Crump

GETTING TO KNOW YOU

Making Friends

Q: HOW DO I MAKE FRIENDS?

1

A: The first step is to look for places where you might find friends. Actually, potential friends are everywhere—in your neighborhood, at school, on your sports team, and at church. You probably already know a lot of kids who could become very good friends.

The best way to make friends is to be friendly. In other words, you should be the kind of person that others will like to have as a friend. Think about what you like in a friend, and be that kind of person to others. This probably will mean showing interest in other people and being a good listener—all of us want friends who will listen carefully to what we say and take us seriously. To have a friend, be a friend!

KEY VERSE: *Do for others what you would like them to do for you. This is a summary of all that is taught in the law and the prophets. (Matthew 7:12)*

RELATED VERSES: *Romans 12:10; Philippians 2:4*

NOTE TO PARENTS: *If your children ask how to make friends, use this opportunity to teach social skills. Try to find out what's behind the question. Perhaps, as their social circles widen, your children may be worried about losing friends. Or they may be feeling lonely. Start by reassuring them that having trouble making friends is a problem that can be solved. They just need to learn how to do it.*

Q: WHEN YOU'RE MAKING FRIENDS, HOW DO YOU KNOW WHAT TO SAY?

2

A: The best way to start a conversation with someone is to ask questions about that person. You can look for visible clues on the person to help you know what to ask. For example, if the person is wearing a hat or shirt of a professional sports team, you could ask about the team. If someone is holding a book, you could ask what it's about. It's important to ask people questions about themselves. Talk about them, not just about yourself. Also, look for ways to compliment people. If you hear about a good grade or honor that someone received, you could say, "Good going!" or "Great job!" If someone did well in a concert, you could say something like, "I really enjoyed your solo." Look for ways to give sincere compliments. Try to make others feel good about themselves.

KEY VERSE: *Kind words are like honey—sweet to the soul and healthy for the body. (Proverbs 16:24)*

RELATED VERSES: *Proverbs 22:11; Romans 15:2*

NOTE TO PARENTS: *You can teach your children how to begin conversations by role-playing with them. This will be fun and will give them valuable practice. Also, be sure to model the above advice in your own relationships with your children and with others.*

Q: I WANT TO HAVE NICE FRIENDS, BUT HOW DO I KNOW IF KIDS ARE NICE?

3

A: You can get an idea of what a person is like by reputation, especially if the reputation is good. For example, if you hear from a lot of people that someone is nice, that's probably a good sign that the person really *is* nice. Sometimes, however, a person's reputation is not always accurate. For example, someone may say that a boy is stuck-up when, instead, he is only shy. Be careful not to judge kids before you know them—give them a chance.

The best way to know if kids are nice is to get to know them yourself. Start talking with them. The Bible teaches that a person's words show what is in that person's heart. If people talk about bad things, swear, or tell dirty jokes, that is a sign of what they are really like. Watch kids in action with others. Pretty soon you will know if they're nice or not.

KEY VERSE: *Many will say they are loyal friends, but who can find one who is really faithful? (Proverbs 20:6)*

RELATED VERSE: *Proverbs 17:17*

NOTE TO PARENTS: *Have fun with this one. Look at magazine pictures and ask your kids what they think the people in the pictures are like. Then you can discuss how looks often deceive and how important it is to get to know a person.*

You may need to help your children identify the types of words and actions that show whether or not someone is nice. Since kids these days are used to hearing bad or unkind words, they may say something like, "Oh, he talks like that, but he's really a nice person." Help your children recognize words as a gauge to a person's heart.

Q: WHERE CAN I FIND SOME FRIENDS?

I'D LIKE TO PUT THIS AD FOR A FRIEND INTO THIS CHURCH BULLETIN, PLEASE.

SOMEONE WHO LIKES HEDGEHOGS, GREEN SLIME & PEANUT BUTTER (swimming pool is an asset!)

4

A: Potential friends are everywhere, usually pretty close by. One of the best places to look for friends is in a group or activity. If you play soccer or sing in choir, for example, you probably will find friends there. Or someone who sits near you in class might turn out to be a good friend. Also consider your church and neighborhood. You might look for someone who needs a friend just as you do. Maybe there's a new family in your neighborhood or church with a child your age. Or maybe you've seen a new student in school. People like that need friends. Perhaps you can be a friend to them.

KEY VERSE: *Anyone who fears you is my friend—anyone who obeys your commandments. (Psalm 119:63)*

RELATED VERSE: *Psalm 55:14*

NOTE TO PARENTS: *Help your children enlarge their friendship circles; plug them in to positive groups. For example, church offers many opportunities for social activities—Bible clubs, choirs, and so on. In addition, you can help by opening your house to other children. Make your home a place where kids want to be.*

Q: WHAT SHOULD I DO IF I'M SCARED TO GO UP TO SOMEONE AND SAY, "HI, DO YOU WANT TO BE MY FRIEND?"

5

A: You don't have to do that. In fact, that's not a very good way to make friends. That question really puts people on the spot, and they don't know how to answer. It's better to go slower and work at getting to know a person. You can do this by asking them questions about themselves. Let friendship happen; don't force it.

KEY VERSE: *Love each other with genuine affection, and take delight in honoring each other. (Romans 12:10)*

NOTE TO PARENTS: *This is another good place to role-play or practice. You can also tell your children how you make friends.*

Q: WHY CAN'T I HAVE EVERYONE AS A FRIEND?

6

A: There are too many kids and not enough time for you to be a good friend to everyone. Actually, there are many different kinds of friendships. Some friends who are very close will be your very good friends. Some kids, however, you will just know by name; they are called acquaintances. Even if you don't know someone's name, you can be friendly to that person. It's good to like everybody and be friendly, but don't expect everyone to like you the same way and to be a really close friend. Friendship takes time. It takes a lot of talking with someone to know someone well. Be friendly with everyone, but work at having a few very close friends. Keep in mind that even Jesus, who loved everyone, had just three very special friends.

KEY VERSE: *Jesus took Peter, James, and John to the top of a mountain. No one else was there. (Mark 9:2)*

RELATED VERSES: *Matthew 26:37-38*

NOTE TO PARENTS: *Children who ask this question may feel insecure, realizing that not everyone wants to be their friend. Explain the various levels of friendship (acquaintance, friend, close friend, very close friend, etc.), and give examples from your life of friends at each level. Some children will easily develop a few close friendships and tend not to socialize beyond them. Others will easily have many friends, but they may not be close friends. Both casual acquaintances and close friends are helpful and bring happiness to our lives. It's natural to lean one way or the other, but we should help our children develop in both areas.*

Q: WHY DO SOME KIDS NOT WANT TO HAVE FRIENDS?

7

A: They may be shy. Or they may be afraid. It can be scary to meet new people if you don't know how. They may be new to the school or neighborhood. And some kids just like to do things by themselves instead of with others. They may have had bad experiences with other kids rejecting them or making fun of them. If this has happened, they may not want to try again. It may seem that some don't want to have friends, but perhaps you just don't know them very well. Maybe you can be a friend to them.

KEY VERSE: *But the time is coming—in fact, it is already here—when you will be scattered, each one going his own way, leaving me alone. Yet I am not alone because the Father is with me. (John 16:32)*

RELATED QUESTIONS: *How does it feel to have no friends? Do loners try to make friends?*

NOTE TO PARENTS: *Maybe your children have been rebuffed in their attempts to befriend other kids. If this is the case, encourage them to continue to be friendly toward those kids but to look for closer friends elsewhere.*

Q: HOW SHOULD I TREAT KIDS WHO ARE DIFFERENT?

8

A: Kids differ in many ways. They may be different races, come from different cultures, or be different sizes. Some children may be mentally or physically challenged. People in a school or neighborhood may even speak different languages. It's never right to make fun of people or ignore them because of those differences. Just because kids are different doesn't mean that they are wrong or to be feared. Think about this: It's God who made the different races and gave people the ability to do things differently. Even if people have different ideas about God, he still wants us to be kind and to respect others. No matter how different kids are, God wants us to treat them in the way we would like to be treated.

KEY VERSE: *The woman was surprised, for Jews refuse to have anything to do with Samaritans. She said to Jesus, "You are a Jew, and I am a Samaritan woman. Why are you asking me for a drink?" (John 4:9)*

RELATED VERSES: *Matthew 25:37-40; Luke 19:1-5*

RELATED QUESTIONS: *Why won't some kids play with kids who are different or who have problems? Why do some kids have to be in wheelchairs?*

NOTE TO PARENTS: *Schools and communities vary. Some are homogenous; others diverse. Every school will have children who are quite different from the others. So be prepared for this question. Also, help your children enjoy and experience the diversity in your community. Take them out for ethnic food. Point out good things in other cultures. Take them to visit special-needs patients in a hospital. The more you help your children experience the differences, the more comfortable they will be with them.*

Q: WHY DO PARENTS NOT LIKE YOUR FRIENDS JUST BECAUSE THEY HAVE GREEN HAIR OR SOMETHING?

MY PARENTS WON'T LET ME BRING MY FRIENDS HOME, SO CAN WE COME TO **YOUR** HOUSE?

9

A: Parents want the best for their children. They know that friends have a big influence. So when they see green hair, they may be surprised or shocked and not know what to think. They know that having green hair may be one way kids express themselves or get attention. But it may also be their way of rebelling against their parents. Your mom and dad probably won't assume that you will want to have green hair too, but they may think that you will pick up your friend's bad attitude. It's not the clothes or hair that your parents don't like; it's what they think the clothes mean to that person. What kind of impression do you give other parents by the way *you* look or act?

KEY VERSE: *Don't copy the behavior and customs of this world, but let God transform you into a new person by changing the way you think. (Romans 12:2)*

RELATED QUESTION: *When kids look tough, why do parents think that they are tough and aren't nice?*

NOTE TO PARENTS: *It's important to get to know your kids' friends. Be careful not to judge them simply by their appearance. Invite the friends to your house. If you notice bad language, bad attitudes, or other negative tendencies, discuss those with your children. Don't make a big issue about appearance unless it becomes evident that it's an outward sign of an inward problem.*

WHY DON'T PARENTS JUST LET YOU PICK YOUR OWN FRIENDS?

10

A: Most parents try to let their children choose their own friends, but some of the choices may not seem very good. Your parents usually know more about your friends' families than you do, and they want you to hang around good and positive moms, dads, brothers, and sisters in other families. Talk this over with your parents. God gave you your parents for a reason. They know you well. Your parents can help you find good friends.

KEY VERSE: *Listen, my child, to what your father teaches you. Don't neglect your mother's teaching. (Proverbs 1:8)*

RELATED VERSES: *Proverbs 13:1; Ephesians 6:1-3*

NOTE TO PARENTS: *Don't be afraid to be involved in helping your children find the right friends. Don't choose for them, but give them guidance. If they really want to befriend someone who is not a good choice for a close friend, that child can still be an acquaintance whom they see from time to time.*

Q: SOMETIMES WHEN I HANG AROUND WITH MY FRIENDS, THEY DO SOMETHING BAD. WHAT SHOULD I DO?

11

A: If the kids you are with begin to talk about or plan something that is not right, tell them not to do it, firmly but nicely. Don't yell or get angry—just explain that what they are doing is wrong. You can suggest doing something else. If that doesn't work, you should leave. If those kids don't want to be friends anymore or if they continue to do things that are wrong, then they aren't very good friends or the type of friends to have. When something like this happens, be sure to discuss it with your parents.

KEY VERSE: *Whoever walks with the wise will become wise; whoever walks with fools will suffer harm. (Proverbs 13:20)*

RELATED VERSES: *John 17:15; Ephesians 5:11; 3 John 1:11*

RELATED QUESTION: *How do you know if you fit in with all the people in your group?*

NOTE TO PARENTS: *Let your children know that they can talk to you about things like this. Tell them you won't assume that they're bad, too, and you are happy to know that they want to do what's right. When they do come to you, emphasize what they did right more than how bad their friends are. Seeking your advice demonstrates the maturity your children have to make the right friendship decisions on their own, with a little guidance from you.*

Q: WHAT SHOULD I DO WHEN MY OLD FRIENDS DON'T LIKE MY NEW FRIENDS?

12

A: You can't control other people's feelings, so you can't make one person like someone else. Maybe your old friends don't know your new friends—you can help them get acquainted. If one group of friends criticizes the other, you can stick up for those who are being criticized. That's the sign of a real friend. Don't let yourself be drawn into rejecting one group of friends for another—it's all right to have more than one group of friends. You can have friends at church, friends at school, friends who are relatives, and friends in your neighborhood.

KEY VERSES: *But when Peter arrived back in Jerusalem, some of the Jewish believers criticized him. "You entered the home of Gentiles and even ate with them!" they said. (Acts 11:2-3)*

RELATED VERSES: *Proverbs 27:10; Acts 11:1-18; Galatians 2:11-16*

RELATED QUESTION: *How do you know your old friends still like you when you have new friends?*

NOTE TO PARENTS: *Friendships change, and that can be tough for children. It's painful to see relationships fade, whatever the reasons. Changes often occur when new children move into a neighborhood. Even greater changes will take place when your children enter middle school and when they begin high school. Encourage your children to learn now not to give in to pressure to reject new friends. Give them suggestions for ways to be friendly to both old and new friends.*

CLOSER THAN A BROTHER

Being a Good Friend

Q: WHAT'S THE DIFFERENCE BETWEEN BEING BEST FRIENDS AND JUST BEING FRIENDS?

13

A: "Best friends" is a way of saying "very close friends." The difference between "very close friends" and others is that you spend a lot of time with very close friends and you can talk to them about lots of things. Very close friends stick with you when you are having problems or are in a bad mood. You can have a lot of friends, but you'll probably have just a few very close friends. You should be careful about the kinds of kids you choose as your very close friends. They should want to please God and do what is right—like you do. It's hard to be close friends with kids if you and they don't see life the same way.

KEY VERSE: *After David had finished talking with Saul, he met Jonathan, the king's son. There was an immediate bond of love between them, and they became the best of friends. (1 Samuel 18:1)*

RELATED VERSES: *Proverbs 27:6, 17*

NOTE TO PARENTS: *Someone may be one of your children's best friends one week and then somebody else's best friend the next. Be available to give advice and support whenever you discover that your children are negotiating friendships. Encourage them to invite Christian friends over, and try to say yes to activities or outings that involve these children. You can be more sparing with other approvals, but don't always say no. And be sure to always explain your reasoning.*

Q: CAN YOU HAVE MORE THAN ONE BEST FRIEND?

14

A: Of course, if *best* really means "best," then the answer is no. Only one can be the absolute best at anything. But *best* friend usually means *very close* friend. In that case, yes, you can have several very close friends. Try not to single out one person as your one and only *best* friend. Calling a person that may make your other close friends feel bad and think that you don't like them. Just because kids aren't your very closest friends doesn't mean that you can't or shouldn't be friendly to them or spend time with them. Who knows, they might become close friends too.

KEY VERSE: *A friend is always loyal, and a brother is born to help in time of need. (Proverbs 17:17)*

RELATED VERSE: *Galatians 6:10*

NOTE TO PARENTS: *We tend to overuse extremes and superlatives like best. Encourage your children to have more than one close friend instead of narrowing down their friendships to one best friend. Also help your children realize that a circle of close friends shouldn't become an exclusive circle of friends.*

Q: MY FRIEND'S PARENTS ARE GETTING A DIVORCE. WHAT CAN I DO?

15

A: Be a good friend—listen to your friend and give your support. Pray for your friend and his or her parents. Remember, you can't do anything about the parents' relationship with each other. They will have to work that out. You probably don't know much about what has been going on in your friend's family, and that's OK. Being a friend means just being there to talk, listen, and care. Right now your friend really needs you.

KEY VERSE: *I would speak in a way that helps you. I would try to take away your grief. (Job 16:5)*

RELATED VERSES: *Job 2:11; Psalm 35:14; Proverbs 27:9*

NOTE TO PARENTS: *When divorce happens to other families, your children may wonder if it will happen to your family. Assure them of your commitment to Christ and to each other, explaining that you intend to remain married—they don't have to worry.*

Q: WHY DO FRIENDS GET MAD AT YOU WHEN YOU TELL THE TRUTH?

16

A: Truth hurts, especially when someone points out something wrong in our life. Sometimes telling the truth to friends can make them feel very uncomfortable. But just because something is true doesn't mean you have to say it. In fact, sometimes you might think that you're "telling the truth" when you're really just bragging. For example, you may find yourself saying something like, "I'm a better singer than you are." Don't do that—don't compare yourself to others. Instead, look for truthful ways to compliment your friends.

You should be sensitive to others' feelings. There's a right time and a wrong time to speak the truth. If you have an important and possibly painful message, wait to tell your friend in private instead of in front of everyone. Also, the *way* you say something means as much as *what* you say. Always remember to be kind and gentle.

KEY VERSE: *Instead, we will hold to the truth in love, becoming more and more in every way like Christ, who is the head of his body, the church. (Ephesians 4:15)*

RELATED VERSES: *2 Samuel 12:1-12; Proverbs 27:6; Ecclesiastes 3:7*

RELATED QUESTION: *Why can't you lie to your friends?*

NOTE TO PARENTS: *This is a good opportunity to explain tact and the loving use of truth versus the hurtful use of truth. Hurtful truths usually are said during an argument. Help your children understand that it's all right to disagree with someone, but we need to disagree agreeably and lovingly.*

WHEN YOU ARE TALKING WITH PEOPLE, HOW DO YOU KNOW THAT THEY ARE ACTUALLY LISTENING TO YOU?

17

A: People who listen carefully to you look at you when you are talking—they don't look at the TV or other people. Also, they usually will comment on what you are saying. If you want to make sure that someone is listening, ask a question from time to time about what you have been saying. You could ask, for example, "What do you think?" If someone says, "What?" or "Huh?", you know that the person has not been listening.

Everyone likes to talk to people who know how to listen. Here are three steps to being a good listener: (1) LOOK—stop what you are doing and look at the person who is talking to you. Give that person all of your attention. (2) LISTEN—concentrate on what the person is saying and try to understand. Don't interrupt. (3) RESPOND—say something related to what the person has been talking about. Comment or ask a question; don't just grunt and change the topic.

What kind of listener are you?

KEY VERSES: *My child, listen to me and treasure my instructions. Tune your ears to wisdom, and concentrate on understanding. (Proverbs 2:1-2)*

RELATED VERSES: *Ezekiel 33:30-31; Luke 19:45-48*

NOTE TO PARENTS: *Consider how well you listen to your children. When you talk with them, be sure to look at them and not interrupt. Then comment on what they are saying. Give them your full attention. Be a good example by following the points mentioned above.*

Q: WHY DO FRIENDS TALK BEHIND YOUR BACK?

18

A: Every person is sinful, so everyone does things that are wrong. Sometimes we even harm the people we love. It hurts when friends do that to each other, but it happens.

Most kids who say bad things about others don't realize that it's wrong and hurtful. They have never learned that they are not only hurting others, they are also hurting themselves by pushing friends away. Some kids give in to pressure from others and go along with what has been said, even if it's about a friend. Many times kids will repeat things they've heard about someone without talking to the person to see if those things are true. This is known as gossiping. Spreading rumors can really hurt people. The Bible says gossiping is wrong—it hurts people and breaks up friendships.

KEY VERSE: *For I am afraid that when I come to visit you I won't like what I find, and then you won't like my response. I am afraid that I will find quarreling, jealousy, outbursts of anger, selfishness, backstabbing, gossip, conceit, and disorderly behavior. (2 Corinthians 12:20)*

RELATED VERSES: *Psalm 41:7; Proverbs 16:28; 18:24; Romans 1:29-30*

RELATED QUESTIONS: *Why do friends tell mean secrets about you? Why can't my friends just tell me everything they know?*

NOTE TO PARENTS: *What kind of example do you set? Be careful not to gossip. A good time to teach your children the difference between gossiping and reporting facts is when they tell you about some trouble between them and another child. Teach your children how to report facts without making judgments.*

Q: WHY WON'T MY FRIEND LET ME PLAY WITH HIS STUFF?

19

A: Your friend may be afraid that his stuff will be broken or misused. Maybe someone recently played with one of his toys and broke it. Remember, the stuff belongs to your friend, so respect his wishes. If you want to play with your friend's things, ask him and promise to take good care of it. If he lets you, show him how careful you can be. If he says no, don't keep asking. Let it go.

KEY VERSE: *Show respect for everyone. Love your Christian brothers and sisters. Fear God. (1 Peter 2:17)*

NOTE TO PARENTS: *Explain to your children that although people are more important than possessions, misusing someone's property can destroy a relationship. The key is to respect the friend. Showing respect to a friend involves respecting that person's property. On the other hand, encourage your children to be willing to share their things. "I'm afraid they might break it" can be an excuse for selfishness.*

Q: WHY CAN'T I GO OVER TO MY BEST FRIEND'S HOUSE VERY OFTEN?

I HAVE SWIMMING LESSONS ON MONDAYS, VIOLIN LESSONS TUESDAYS, GYMNASTICS ON WEDNESDAYS, CUBS ON THURSDAYS, AND FRIDAY IS MY INTERNET NIGHT. BUT I CAN FIT YOU IN BETWEEN A DENTIST APPOINTMENT AND MY PAPER ROUTE SATURDAY MORNING... I ALWAYS MAKE TIME FOR MY BEST FRIEND!

20

A: If your parents are saying that you can't go over to your friend's house very often, ask them why. Maybe they don't know your friend very well. You can fix that by having your friend come to your house. If your friend doesn't invite you very often, maybe it's because the parents won't allow it. They may have several reasons, so don't blame your friend. Perhaps your friend is busy with other activities and doesn't have much free time.

Of course, it may be that you want to go over to your friend's house every day. If that's the case, your parents probably don't want you to "wear out your welcome."

KEY VERSE: *Don't visit your neighbors too often, or you will wear out your welcome. (Proverbs 25:17)*

RELATED QUESTION: *Why are sleep-overs better than just sleeping by yourself?*

NOTE TO PARENTS: *Teach your children some of the guidelines for moderate and mutually fair hospitality. Double-check your children's knowledge and performance of good manners. Remind them that polite, courteous, and helpful people are pleasant to be around and usually get invited back.*

Q: WHY DON'T MY PARENTS LET ME GO TO SPECIAL PLACES WITH MY FRIENDS?

21

A: What are some places that are special to you? The movie theater? The mall? An arcade? An ice-cream shop? Sometimes a certain place may seem special, but your parents know that bad things can happen there. They will want to know if any adults will be present if you go there, because even a safe place can become dangerous quickly. Because your parents love you, they want to protect you so you won't get hurt or get into trouble. This means they probably won't let you go to many places by yourself or just with your friends. When your parents do let you go to special places, be extra careful to be responsible and obedient. Your parents will probably allow you to do more as they see you becoming more responsible.

KEY VERSE: *Obey your spiritual leaders and do what they say. Their work is to watch over your souls, and they know they are accountable to God. Give them reason to do this joyfully and not with sorrow. That would certainly not be for your benefit. (Hebrews 13:17)*

RELATED VERSE: *Proverbs 22:3*

RELATED QUESTIONS: *Why do other people get special privileges and I don't? Why do friends go to more special places than our family does?*

NOTE TO PARENTS: *As spiritual leaders for our children, sometimes we can be overprotective. Eventually, however, we have to let them go. This process begins when children are young. Show them that you love and trust them by allowing them to venture out to select places with their friends. But make sure that these places are safe and supervised or chaperoned by responsible adults.*

Q: WHY SHOULD WE ALWAYS HAVE TO RESCUE OUR FRIENDS WHEN THEY GET IN TROUBLE?

FROG CATCHING CLUB
SMELLY SWAMP BRANCH

22

A: God says that we should help those who are in trouble, even our *enemies*. That's what it means to love, and it's how we can show others God's love. You can help your friends when they are in trouble. That's being a very good friend to them. However, there's a limit to what you can do—parents and other adults may need to help. You shouldn't lie for friends or make excuses for them. Sometimes letting friends learn to solve their own problems is the best thing to do.

KEY VERSE: *The greatest love is shown when people lay down their lives for their friends. (John 15:13)*

RELATED VERSES: *Psalm 107:6; Proverbs 19:19*

RELATED QUESTION: *How can I help when my friend is grounded at home?*

NOTE TO PARENTS: *It's good for your children to learn how to help others, but don't be afraid to step in when friends seem to be taking advantage of your children's goodwill. Kids want to help their friends and will automatically try to defend and protect a child who is in trouble for doing something wrong. Help your children understand that at times they need to rescue their friends, but at other times it is better to let those kids experience the consequences of their actions.*

Q: WHAT SHOULD I DO IF MY FRIEND TURNS ON A SHOW THAT I'M NOT ALLOWED TO WATCH?

23

A: You can explain that you're not allowed to watch that show and ask your friend to change the channel. If that doesn't work, you can excuse yourself and go to another room or even go home, telling your friend in a nice way how you feel. You can explain why your parents don't want you to watch that show. This may help your friend make wiser choices when it comes to watching television. You may also want to explain that your parents will get very upset if they find out—it's just not worth the risk. Then you can suggest something else to do.

KEY VERSES: *I will refuse to look at anything vile and vulgar. I hate all crooked dealings; I will have nothing to do with them. I will reject perverse ideas and stay away from every evil. (Psalm 101:3-4)*

RELATED VERSES: *Proverbs 1:10; 1 Corinthians 10:13; 2 Timothy 2:22*

RELATED QUESTION: *Why do kids sometimes get nightmares from the movies they watch?*

NOTE TO PARENTS: *Regulating your children's TV watching is easier said than done. Talk about specific TV shows and videos with your children. Let them know your expectations and reasons. Also assure them that at any age and at any time they can call you if a situation gets out of hand, and you will come pick them up.*

UPS AND DOWNS

Handling Friendship Difficulties

Q: WHY DO FRIENDS LET EACH OTHER DOWN?

24

A: Sometimes we expect too much from our friends; then we feel let down when they don't come through for us. Some of our friends may be having a bad day and are working on their own problems. At those times your friends will find it difficult to help you. At other times your friends may not even be aware of your problems. They may not know that they have let you down. It's all right to express your disappointment and explain to them how you feel. When you talk to your friends in a nice way about how you feel, it will help you and them learn how to be better friends.

KEY VERSE: *The godly give good advice to their friends; the wicked lead them astray. (Proverbs 12:26)*

RELATED VERSES: *Proverbs 20:6; Mark 14:44-50; 2 Timothy 4:16*

RELATED QUESTION: *Why do my friends let me down when I'm honest with them?*

NOTE TO PARENTS: *This provides a good opportunity to explain that friendships have ups and downs. That's normal. It's also a good time to encourage your children to have several good friends and not just one best friend.*

IF A FRIEND ASKS ME TO KEEP A PROMISE AND IT'S SOMETHING WRONG, SHOULD I DO IT?

25

A: You don't have to keep a promise if someone will be hurt by it. If your friend says something like, "I'm going to tell you something, but you have to promise not to tell anyone else," you can say, "I can't promise to do that if what you are going to tell me is wrong." Let your friend know that you can't make any promise that goes against your promise to God to obey him. It's better to let your friend know up front what promises you will keep. Then, when you do promise something, be sure to keep your promise.

KEY VERSE: *Take no part in the worthless deeds of evil and darkness; instead, rebuke and expose them. (Ephesians 5:11)*

RELATED QUESTION: *When friends break promises, don't they want to do what they said? or do they sometimes forget?*

NOTE TO PARENTS: *You can model appropriate keeping of promises with your children. Be sure to keep the secrets they share whenever you can. Let your children know, however, that if someone will be hurt, you won't keep quiet.*

Q: WHY CAN'T MY BEST FRIEND STAY HERE WITH ME AND NOT MOVE AWAY?

26

A: It hurts when friends leave. It hurts your friend even more because, although you are losing one person, your friend is leaving almost everyone familiar. Your friend's family probably had a good reason for moving; for example, a parent may have received a promotion or a new job. Perhaps you can get your friend's new address and continue your friendship as pen pals or e-mail pals. Many families who move away from a city come back to visit. If you stay in touch, you will know when your friend is coming and possibly be able to get together.

Someday *you* might have to move. One of the facts of life is that situations don't stay the same, so it's important to learn how to deal with change.

KEY VERSES: *When he had finished speaking, he knelt and prayed with them. They wept aloud as they embraced him in farewell, sad most of all because he had said that they would never see him again. Then they accompanied him down to the ship. (Acts 20:36-38)*

RELATED VERSE: *2 Timothy 1:4*

RELATED QUESTION: *Is it OK to feel sad when friends leave?*

NOTE TO PARENTS: *Because society has become very mobile, some of your children's friends will probably move away. Instead of focusing on the losses, help your children learn to value the friendships they have. Encourage your children to keep in touch with their long-distance friends through E-mail, phone calls, and letters. If your family will be moving, pray together about the new friendships that will be formed in your new neighborhood, church, and school.*

Q: WHY WOULD YOUR FRIENDS EXPECT YOU TO LIE FOR THEM?

27

A: Some people think that friends should do anything for them—even lie. But that's not part of friendship. More important than doing what your friends want or expect is doing what God wants. That's what you should consider first. Your relationship with God should be your most important friendship, and God says that lying is wrong.

KEY VERSE: *Do not steal. Do not cheat one another. Do not lie. (Leviticus 19:11)*

RELATED VERSE: *Ephesians 4:25*

RELATED QUESTIONS: *Why do we lie to keep friends out of trouble? Why can't my friend just not do anything wrong so I don't have to lie for her?*

NOTE TO PARENTS: *Help your children know that a lie is the "intent to deceive." It's intentionally keeping quiet about the truth. In other words, a lie is not limited to saying words that are untrue. Saying nothing or saying the right words in the wrong way can also be lying.*

Q: WHY DON'T YOUR FRIENDS LIKE YOU JUST FOR WHO YOU ARE?

28

A: Usually they do. That's probably what caused you to become friends in the first place—they like who you are. At times, however, friends may want to change something about who you are that's different from who *they* are. They may want you to stop doing things that are different from what *they* do. One of the great parts of friendship is getting to know someone who is completely different from you. God didn't make any two people alike, so learn to appreciate how your friends are different.

KEY VERSES: *Just as our bodies have many parts and each part has a special function, so it is with Christ's body. We are all parts of his one body, and each of us has different work to do. And since we are all one body in Christ, we belong to each other, and each of us needs all the others. (Romans 12:4-5)*

RELATED VERSE: *Romans 12:2*

RELATED QUESTION: *Why do friends expect you to do things just the way they do?*

NOTE TO PARENTS: *Kids face pressure to conform. Help them be true to themselves without being weird. Encourage your children to accept constructive criticism and to change when their friends bring up something that they perhaps should change.*

Q: WHY DO YOU HAVE TO DO WHATEVER YOUR FRIENDS WANT, OR THEY GET MAD?

29

A: It's natural to want to have our own way, so your friends may get mad at you when you don't do something they want you to do. That's not the way friendship should work, however. Sometimes a compromise is the way for everyone to be happy. Other times it means taking turns doing what each friend wants. If friends always want things their way or if they get angry with you when you don't conform, talk with them about it. If your friends are pressuring you to do something that you aren't comfortable with or that is dangerous or wrong, then you probably should find a new set of friends.

KEY VERSES: *Keep away from angry, short-tempered people, or you will learn to be like them and endanger your soul. (Proverbs 22:24-25)*

RELATED VERSES: *Ecclesiastes 7:9; 1 Corinthians 13:4-5*

NOTE TO PARENTS: *Help your children think about times when it's appropriate to give in to others and times when it's important not to give in to them, even if they get angry.*

Q:

WHY CAN'T FRIENDS JUST GET ALONG INSTEAD OF FIGHTING AND ARGUING WITH EACH OTHER?

30

A: You'd think that friends would get along great *all the time*. But conflicts happen because everyone has ups and downs; sometimes a person is just in a bad mood. No two people agree on everything all the time. In any disagreement, however, instead of fighting and arguing, the people should talk it through and work together to solve the problem. If your friends are always fighting and arguing, you can be a good example yourself and help them resolve the issue. And you can keep from following the bad example of your friends by spending more time with kids who are learning to get along with each other.

KEY VERSE: *Beginning a quarrel is like opening a floodgate, so drop the matter before a dispute breaks out. (Proverbs 17:14)*

RELATED VERSE: *Proverbs 20:3*

RELATED QUESTIONS: *Why can't you tell on a friend without your friendship breaking up? What do you do if friends fight and argue with each other? Should you leave if your friends are in a fight?*

NOTE TO PARENTS: *A good place to teach children how to get along with others is at home as they deal with their brothers and sisters. Enabling your children to work out sibling conflicts takes time. But it's an important way for them to develop the skills they need to get along with each other and with their friends. When arguments occur, teach your children how to "fight fair." Let them know it is possible to disagree with someone without screaming, yelling, and calling them names.*

Q: WHY DO MY FRIENDS BREAK THEIR PROMISES TO ME?

31

A: Only God is perfect and will never break his promises. Most people who make promises intend to keep them, but they may forget. Or circumstances may change. For example, a friend may say that you can visit her anytime, but a baby brother arrives and the family limits the number of visitors for a while. Sometimes people make promises that are almost impossible to keep—like saying, "I will never get angry with you." If a friend breaks a promise to you, let that person know how you feel, but try to be forgiving and understanding. Ask God to help you make only promises that you can keep. Then do your best to keep those promises.

KEY VERSE: *It is better to say nothing than to promise something that you don't follow through on. (Ecclesiastes 5:5)*

RELATED VERSES: *1 Kings 8:23; Proverbs 17:17*

RELATED QUESTION: *Instead of making promises they'll break, why won't friends just be quiet?*

NOTE TO PARENTS: *When children discover the promise concept, they can overuse it to make pacts with their friends. Help your children understand that promises are important and that we should say what we mean and do what we say.*

Q:

WHEN ONE OF MY FRIENDS IS PICKING ON SOMEONE, WHAT SHOULD I DO?

32

A:
Don't join in. Maybe you could change the subject or get your friend to do something else instead. If things get bad, remember that no one has the right to touch or hit another person if that person doesn't want them to. Adults who hit people can go to jail for their actions. It's against the law, and it's not the way God wants us to treat others. If your friend's actions involve pushing or hitting of any kind, tell him to stop. Then go tell an adult immediately.

KEY VERSE: *Dear friend, don't let this bad example influence you. Follow only what is good. (3 John 1:11)*

RELATED VERSES: *Luke 6:37; 1 Corinthians 13:4-5*

RELATED QUESTIONS: *Why do people have to tease and not be friends? If a friend is mean to other people, should I be his or her best friend?*

NOTE TO PARENTS: *This is an answer that's easy to say, but hard to do. Your child may need backup from you. With all the violence that children see on television and in movies, they may think that mild physical abuse is part of life. Respect for others begins at home. Teach your children to respect others' rights for safety. Never allow any touching with the intent to harm.*

Q: IF MY FRIENDS IGNORE ME, SHOULD I IGNORE THEM?

33

A: No—we should do what is right toward others even if they do wrong to us. This is difficult, but God expects us to do what is right regardless of what others do. Over time, our friendliness may win the other kids over. Sometimes we should just overlook what people do to us, but we should not ignore them as people. Probably the best way to act toward someone who is ignoring you is the exact opposite. You can go right up to the person and say something like this: "I'm sorry if I have upset you. Can we talk about it?"

KEY VERSE: *Never pay back evil for evil to anyone. Do things in such a way that everyone can see you are honorable. (Romans 12:17)*

RELATED VERSE: *Psalm 66:20*

RELATED QUESTIONS: *Sometimes people I talk to listen for a second, then the next minute they're ignoring me. Why do people do this? When friends aren't friendly anymore, should I ask them, "Why are you ignoring me?"*

NOTE TO PARENTS: *This issue can be a crisis for children. You may say, "Just ignore anyone who ignores you." But the hurt will still be there. Friendships change over time, and even the strongest ones experience stress. Talking with someone who doesn't want to talk is not a natural thing to do. However, if you can help your children through it a couple of times until they see positive results, they will develop it as a life habit.*

Q: WHY DO SOME PEOPLE WANT TO BE FRIENDS ONE DAY AND NOT THE NEXT?

34

A: Learning how to be a good friend takes time and effort. Your friends may not realize that the way they are behaving is wrong. Nicely talk with them about it and how it makes you feel. Explain that you would like to know you can count on your friends every day.

It is possible that some kids may *seem* like they're changing their mind about being friends, but they may just be having a bad day. Or they may be spending time that day with another friend. If that's the case, don't worry; they are still your friends.

KEY VERSE: *Never abandon a friend. (Proverbs 27:10)*

NOTE TO PARENTS: *Sometimes children can be possessive about friendships and want to monopolize a person's time and attention. But that will suffocate any friendship. If you think that's happening, help your child understand the importance of developing other friendships as well.*

Q:

WHAT CAN I DO WHEN ONE OF MY BEST FRIENDS USED TO LIKE ME, BUT NOW HE HATES ME?

35

A: First, try to find out what happened. Did you do something to hurt your friend's feelings? If you find out that you did, say that you're sorry. Pray about the situation and ask God for wisdom. Remember, however, that there just may not be a good reason—people change, and you may have lost a friend. Don't try to get even and don't decide to dislike the person back. You can still be nice and pray for your old friend, but be sure to find other friends.

KEY VERSE: *My friends scorn me, but I pour out my tears to God. (Job 16:20)*

RELATED VERSE: *Proverbs 18:19*

RELATED QUESTION: *If kids don't want to be friends anymore, is it OK to just forget about them?*

NOTE TO PARENTS: *Children will often use the word hate when referring to a former friend. What they usually mean is that they are upset with the person. A number of things can spoil a friendship. When relationships sour, there's a tendency to try to "get even." Instead, encourage your children to see this as a good opportunity to become more like Jesus, showing kindness even when it's not returned.*

ROCKY ROAD

Learning to Get Along with Others

Q: WHY ARE SOME KIDS SO MESSY?

A MESSY ROOM IS A SIGN OF CREATIVE GENIUS!

CLONE MASTER

36

A: Kids are different. Some are neat, some are messy, and some are in between. Also, every family is different; some keep their homes much neater than others. So a person who grows up in a messy home may tend to be messy. It's good to be tidy and organized, and hopefully your messy friends will learn this as they grow up. But we shouldn't expect everyone to have everything perfectly in order all the time. While a messy person can be frustrating for someone who is neat, we should remember that being neat is not the most important thing in life. If some people aren't as neat as we are, that doesn't mean that they're bad—just different.

KEY VERSE: *Are we not all children of the same Father? Are we not all created by the same God? (Malachi 2:10)*

RELATED QUESTIONS: *Why do kids lose so many things? If my friends are messy, should I try to help them out or remind them to pick up after themselves?*

NOTE TO PARENTS: *It's easy to get into the habit of seeing others' weaknesses. This habit will frustrate us and divide friends. Help your children work on their own weaknesses and focus on others' strengths. This habit will mature them and strengthen their friendships.*

Q: WHY DO SOME KIDS GET THEIR OWN WAY WHEN THEY CRY AND GET ANGRY?

37

A: Some adults give in when children cry, pout, whine, or throw tantrums. The adults let those children get what they want. Kids who have been treated that way think they can always get what they want by acting like that. But someday those actions won't work. Can you imagine adults falling to the floor in a store, crying loudly, and beating the floor just because the store didn't have what they wanted? It's much better to learn as children to talk things through, be cooperative, and not try to get our way all the time.

KEY VERSES: *So Samson's wife came to him in tears and said, "You don't love me; you hate me! You have given my people a riddle, but you haven't told me the answer." "I haven't even given the answer to my father or mother,"* he replied. *"Why should I tell you?" So she cried whenever she was with him and kept it up for the rest of the celebration. At last, on the seventh day, he told her the answer because of her persistent nagging. Then she gave the answer to the young men. (Judges 14:16-17)*

RELATED QUESTION: *Why do some kids always want their own way?*

NOTE TO PARENTS: *If your children point out that some friends get their way by throwing tantrums, help your kids understand that every home is unique. You are doing your best before God to be a good parent to your family in your home. No one should worry about whether or not other families are different or better. Talk about the fact that when someone in your family is disappointed over something, everyone can get together to work out a happy alternative.*

Q: WHY DO SOME KIDS ALWAYS TRY TO BE FIRST?

38

A: They're selfish. And, by the way, that's part of the sinful, human nature. *All* people tend to be selfish. Only God can help us be unselfish and think of others—we have to depend on him. Kids who always try to be first may be trying to feel better about themselves. They may feel that they are important and valuable because they won a game or got to be first in line. But God says that each person is valuable and important to him, even those who come in last. When we know how much God loves and cares for us, we can let others go first.

KEY VERSE: *And so it is, that many who are first now will be last then; and those who are last now will be first then. (Matthew 20:16)*

RELATED VERSES: *Philippians 2:3-4; James 3:16*

NOTE TO PARENTS: *We should encourage our children to do their best, and it's certainly not wrong to win a game or contest. The problem comes when winning becomes everything. In small matters, like lining up for the drinking fountain, help your children learn that God is happier when we don't try to be first all the time.*

Q: SHOULD I STAND UP FOR MYSELF AROUND PUSHY KIDS?

39

A: Yes, tell them how you feel. Be firm, but don't yell and lose your cool. The Bible says that a gentle answer will help calm a situation. Staying cool and being as nice as you can is your best chance for a good outcome. Sometimes this won't work, and you'll be tempted to fight. But don't do it—walk away instead. If kids get pushy, tell an adult.

KEY VERSE: *A gentle answer turns away wrath, but harsh words stir up anger. (Proverbs 15:1)*

RELATED VERSES: *Nehemiah 6:8-9; Matthew 5:39*

RELATED QUESTIONS: *Why do I get upset around friends who are pushy? Should I tell pushy kids not to be pushy because no one likes it?*

NOTE TO PARENTS: *Many parents tell their children to stand up for themselves and push back. But the Bible says to honor others and to turn the other cheek. This doesn't mean that children should become doormats. They should stand up for their rights but do it respectfully. They shouldn't fight.*

Q: WHY DO SOME KIDS JUST HAVE TO TALK IN CLASS? WHY CAN'T THEY WAIT UNTIL RECESS?

40

A: Some are not mature enough to wait. Babies can't wait for anything. They want to be changed or fed or moved *now!* As children get older, however, they learn to have patience and do things at the right time, not whenever they feel like it. They also learn that the whole world doesn't revolve around them and that other people have needs too. Some kids, however, take a little longer than they should to learn these lessons.

Some kids might talk in class because they're afraid they will forget what they have to say. You could suggest that they write a reminder note to themselves to talk about it at recess or between classes.

KEY VERSE: *Don't talk too much, for it fosters sin. Be sensible and turn off the flow! (Proverbs 10:19)*

RELATED VERSES: *Proverbs 20:19; Ecclesiastes 3:1, 7; James 3:2*

RELATED QUESTIONS: *If kids talk during class, should I tell them it's not polite? When the teacher asks a student a question, why do some other kids always call out the answer?*

NOTE TO PARENTS: *If your children talk too much, encourage them to work on this. Discuss possible solutions with their teachers.*

Q: WHY DO KIDS WRECK MY THINGS FOR NO REASON?

41

A: Some kids are careless, and they break things by accident. Some are stronger than they realize and may not know what they are doing. Of course, some may be mean and break your things to hurt you. Some have never learned to take care of other people's property. Let your friends know that you expect them to be careful with your things. You don't have to let kids play with your toys if you know those kids don't care how they handle your things. You don't have to let people into your room if you know they don't care if they mess it up. Be careful, however, not to overreact to a small incident or an accident. Sharing is an important part of friendship.

KEY VERSE: *Let everyone see that you are considerate in all you do. (Philippians 4:5)*

RELATED VERSE: *Ephesians 4:2*

RELATED QUESTIONS: *Do some kids wreck things because they think they're not going to get caught? If friends lose or break my things, why can't I just make them replace those things?*

NOTE TO PARENTS: *Some kids may be mean and cruel. You have to help your children draw the line between sharing and protecting their stuff from careless kids. Be careful what you teach about ownership. Teach your children to respect others' ownership but also to be willing to share what they own.*

Q: WHY DO SOME KIDS ACT TOUGH?

42

A: Usually kids who act tough are trying hard to feel good about themselves. They want everyone to look up to them the way people look up to entertainment or sports celebrities. Tough kids might be nice if they would just start being themselves. And kids who act important would have a lot more friends if they didn't pretend to be better than everyone else. The best person to be is yourself. Then when people like you, you will know that they like you for who you are and not for a pretend image that you are trying to have.

KEY VERSE: *Live in harmony with each other. Don't try to act important, but enjoy the company of ordinary people. And don't think you know it all! (Romans 12:16)*

RELATED VERSES: *Luke 18:9-14; Romans 12:3; 1 Corinthians 4:7; Galatians 2:6*

RELATED QUESTION: *Do kids try to act tough just to attract attention?*

NOTE TO PARENTS: *All kids need attention, and they need to feel good about themselves. We should look for ways to affirm our children, always being ready to give them positive feedback. Don't be afraid that this will make them act important. Instead, children who are confident that they are loved, accepted, and special to their families as well as to God find it much easier to act natural. They know it's OK to be themselves.*

Q: WHY DO SOME KIDS SAY BAD THINGS ABOUT OTHERS?

43

A: They think it's fun. They might be jealous of other kids or angry with them. They might be in competition with them. Or they may not have learned yet that it's unkind. Whatever the reason, it's not right to say bad things about people, to call them names, to spread rumors, or to make fun of others. Unfortunately a lot of humor these days is based on making fun of someone. But laughing at someone is a cruel way to joke around. Don't do it. A good rule to follow is to make sure that everything you say about people will make them feel good. Pretend that they are present to hear what you're saying about them, even if they're not.

KEY VERSE: *They must not speak evil of anyone, and they must avoid quarreling. Instead, they should be gentle and show true humility to everyone. (Titus 3:2)*

RELATED VERSES: *Matthew 12:36; 1 Peter 4:4*

RELATED QUESTIONS: *What should I do if someone says bad things about my friend? When kids talk bad about others, does it always mean they don't like those people?*

NOTE TO PARENTS: *Kids can be cruel to each other. Their cutting remarks often relate to a physical characteristic or other superficial attribute, such as clothing. In addition to helping your children see how unkind it is to put others down, encourage them to look beyond the superficial to the real person. Remember that your children are listening when you talk about others. Making cutting remarks and put-down jokes is a bad habit, and using sarcasm is a destructive disciplinary tool. Make your home a safe place where your children and their friends feel welcomed and affirmed. You may want to add "saying only kind things about people" to your list of family rules.*

Q: WHY ARE SOME KIDS BULLIES?

44

A: They are very selfish and care more about themselves than others. Usually bullies are bigger and stronger than other kids and can take advantage of them. They have learned to get what they want by force. Bullies come in all ages. You can find them in many places in the grown-up world as well as on the playground. No one should get away with bullying others. If you see it or get bullied yourself, tell a teacher, the principal, or your parents right away.

KEY VERSES: *Goliath walked out toward David with his shield bearer ahead of him, sneering in contempt at this ruddy-faced boy. (1 Samuel 17:41-42)*

RELATED VERSE: *Ecclesiastes 4:1*

RELATED QUESTIONS: *What should I do if a bully pushes me around all the time? When someone is being a bully, should I complain to a teacher or adult?*

NOTE TO PARENTS: *If your child is being bullied by someone at school, talk to the teacher. If it's someone in the neighborhood, talk to the parent. Your child does not have to endure cruelty from a bully.*

Q: SHOULD I STICK UP FOR SOMEONE WHO'S BEING BULLIED?

45

A: Yes, always stick up for the person who is being hurt, not the one doing the hurting. If there is a big, strong bully at your school or in your neighborhood, you may want to encourage your friends to stay together in a group to be safer. Be sure to tell an adult about the situation too. Let this person know if extra adult supervision is needed on your school playground. If kids don't feel safe walking home from school, parents may be able to take turns giving rides.

KEY VERSE: *I say to the rest of you, dear brothers and sisters, never get tired of doing good. (2 Thessalonians 3:13)*

RELATED VERSES: *Proverbs 21:3; 2 Corinthians 8:21*

RELATED QUESTION: *Should I tell the bully's parents what he's doing?*

NOTE TO PARENTS: *Encourage your child to inform a caring adult about bully action. This could be a coach, a teacher, a parent, a principal, or another caring adult.*

Q:

IF YOU KNOW A FRIEND IS GOING TO DO SOMETHING WRONG, SHOULD YOU TRY TO STOP THE PERSON?

46

A: Yes, definitely. First, try to talk your friend out of doing what is wrong. Explain that you care about him or her and that's why you want to help. Use your friendship to encourage this friend into doing what is right instead of wrong. If he or she won't listen, tell your parents. If you are present when your friend starts to do what is wrong, leave immediately.

KEY VERSE: *Don't think only about your own affairs, but be interested in others, too, and what they are doing. (Philippians 2:4)*

RELATED VERSE: *2 Timothy 4:2*

RELATED QUESTIONS: *What should I do if I have a friend who does wrong things all the time? If my friends do wrong things, should I tell an adult even if I lose those friends?*

NOTE TO PARENTS: *Two kids can handle many issues without outside help. On the other hand, a "wrong" may be destructive and involve dangerous actions such as drinking, experimenting with drugs, vandalism, or shoplifting. In those situations, adults should be involved as soon as possible. Help your children understand the difference.*

Q: WHAT SHOULD I DO WHEN KIDS ARE MEAN TO ME?

47

A: This will be difficult, but you should be kind to them no matter how mean they are to you. Also, you should pray for them. That's what God expects his people to do. God's way always works out best. You may think that you'll feel better by getting even, but you won't. If you respond God's way, you'll feel better about yourself, and you may even help those kids change when they see your good example. If you have to, avoid them. Don't let their meanness get to you. If they threaten to hurt you physically, you should tell an adult right away.

KEY VERSES: *If your enemies are hungry, feed them. If they are thirsty, give them something to drink, and they will be ashamed of what they have done to you. Don't let evil get the best of you, but conquer evil by doing good. (Romans 12:20-21)*

RELATED VERSES: *1 Peter 2:21-23*

RELATED QUESTIONS: *Do you have to walk away to avoid fights? If someone punches me, what should I do?*

NOTE TO PARENTS: *Every child experiences unkind behavior. "Being mean" can involve anything from name-calling and taunting to hurting someone physically. Sometimes kids feel sad or even guilty about being mistreated and, therefore, won't mention it. So it's important that from time to time you ask your children how people are treating them at school and in the neighborhood.*

Q: WHY IS IT SO HARD TO LOVE YOUR ENEMIES?

48

A: It is very difficult to love enemies because it's not natural. It's the opposite of how everyone around us seems to be behaving. When people hurt us, we want to get back at them because we are human. When people don't like us or act mean toward us, it's natural not to like them. But Jesus tells us to love our enemies, and he promises to give us the strength to do it. "Loving" enemies doesn't necessarily mean having warm feelings about them. It means acting in a loving way toward them, treating them the way Jesus would—praying for them, being kind to them, and so on.

KEY VERSE: *But I say, love your enemies! Pray for those who persecute you! (Matthew 5:44)*

RELATED VERSES: *Luke 6:35-37; Romans 12:17-21*

RELATED QUESTION: *How do you love someone who hates you?*

NOTE TO PARENTS: *Here's another place where you can be a positive example for your children. They are watching you. How do you react when people cut you off in traffic, yell at you, or accuse you falsely? Pray for God's help to respond in love.*

Q: WHEN KIDS TEASE ME, IS IT OK TO TEASE THEM BACK?

49

A: There's a difference between fun teasing and mean teasing. Sometimes kids say nonsense things about each other, not meaning to hurt anyone's feelings. That's OK. When kids tease you in a mean way, however, don't tease them back. Try to ignore them if possible. Just stay quiet. This won't be easy because it's natural to want to say something back to hurt them. If you can, be kind to them. Jesus calls this "turning the other cheek." If a certain group of kids seems to tease you all the time, don't go near those kids. If they call you names, remind yourself that the names do not describe the real you. God knows you, and he says you're special.

KEY VERSE: *Don't repay evil for evil. Don't retaliate when people say unkind things about you. Instead, pay them back with a blessing. That is what God wants you to do, and he will bless you for it. (1 Peter 3:9)*

RELATED VERSES: *Matthew 5:39; 1 Peter 2:21-23*

RELATED QUESTION: *Why do some kids like to tease others?*

NOTE TO PARENTS: *Words can hurt, can't they? They can hurt you, and they can hurt your children. Words can cut and wound deeper than "sticks and stones." Be prepared to heal some word wounds.*

Q: WHY DON'T OTHER KIDS EVER DO WHAT I SAY?

50

A: Do you like to tell others what to do? Do you always want things your way? If that's the case, kids may start ignoring you. Or perhaps some kids don't know you well enough to listen to your suggestions. Your good friends who know you and like you will probably take your ideas and suggestions seriously if you're not too bossy.

Remember, though, no one *has* to do what you say or suggest. You need to learn how to present your ideas in a way that others will want to go along with you. If you support your friends when they have good suggestions, those kids will be a lot easier to convince when you have a good idea.

KEY VERSES: *The next day, as Moses was out visiting his people again, he saw two Hebrew men fighting. "What are you doing, hitting your neighbor like that?" Moses said to the one in the wrong. "Who do you think you are?" the man replied. "Who appointed you to be our prince and judge?" (Exodus 2:13-14)*

RELATED VERSES: *2 Corinthians 1:24; 1 Peter 5:3*

NOTE TO PARENTS: *Children don't develop great social and communication skills automatically. They do, however, often act like their parents. Therefore, if your children talk too much or boss others around, they may have learned that at home. Model and teach good listening skills, and help your children learn how to explain their ideas and suggestions clearly.*

THE "IN" CROWD

Fitting In at School

Q: WHY DO SOME KIDS DRESS SO WEIRD?

51

A: They may like to do it. Actually, their clothes may seem weird to you but not to them. Of course, some kids wear loud and different clothes to be noticed. They want to get a reaction, to get attention. Some kids whose clothes seem weird may be copying musicians or other celebrities who they think are cool. Others may look different just because they don't have enough money to dress in style. Remember not to judge people by the way they dress.

KEY VERSES: *Everything [the Pharisees] do is for show. On their arms they wear extra wide prayer boxes with Scripture verses inside, and they wear extra long tassels on their robes. They enjoy the attention they get on the streets. (Matthew 23:5, 7)*

RELATED VERSE: *1 Samuel 16:7; Matthew 3:4*

RELATED QUESTION: *What should I wear at school?*

NOTE TO PARENTS: *Remember, clothes don't make the person. This cuts both ways. A wonderful person may be dressed in weird clothes. Conversely, a rotten person can hide in the latest styles. It's easy to judge people by their appearance. Be careful to set a good example in this area.*

Q:

SOMETIMES I'M AFRAID TO GO TO SCHOOL. WHAT SHOULD I DO?

52

A: Talk to your parents about your fears. They will help. If there's a specific reason why you are afraid, tell them about it. Teachers and school counselors can also help. You may want to go to school with a friend. This friend can encourage you, pray for you, and give you moral support. Also, you can ask Christian friends, such as your Sunday school teacher and pastor, to pray for you. They can pray also that God will take care of the situation that is causing you to be afraid.

KEY VERSE: *I am holding you by your right hand—I, the Lord your God. And I say to you, "Do not be afraid. I am here to help you." (Isaiah 41:13)*

RELATED VERSES: *Psalm 56:3; Isaiah 26:3; 41:10; Philippians 4:6-7*

NOTE TO PARENTS: *Find out why your child is afraid. The first answer may not be the real reason. Instead of telling your son or daughter to be tough, take time to talk it through and find out what's really happening. A bully may be lurking. Kids may be making fun of your child's clothes or looks. Or your child may be afraid of failing. After determining the cause, you can pray about it together and work toward a solution.*

Q: WHY DO KIDS ALWAYS WANT TO DRESS ACCORDING TO DIFFERENT FADS?

A: They want to fit in, to look like everyone else. Advertisers spend tons of money to make it seem as if everyone should wear certain clothes. Or a famous person might wear an outfit that looks good, and everyone starts buying a similar outfit. That's how fads get started. Soon it seems as though everyone is wearing the same styles and colors. But fads don't last very long. You don't have to dress in every new fad. Many clothing styles are classic and always seem to be in style. You can ask your parents to help you choose the right clothes to wear.

KEY VERSE: *Everything is so weary and tiresome! No matter how much we see, we are never satisfied. No matter how much we hear, we are not content. (Ecclesiastes 1:8)*

RELATED VERSES: *1 Corinthians 7:31; 1 John 2:16-17*

RELATED QUESTION: *Why do kids always follow the newest fad?*

NOTE TO PARENTS: *Let your children know that it's all right to wear the latest styles as long as they aren't too extreme. However, you'll want to point out that kids can be stylish without being faddish. Explain that fashion fads usually look pretty silly a few years later. To prove this point, find some pictures of fads from twenty years ago, or show photos of yourself as a kid.*

Q: WHY DOES EVERYBODY WANT TO DO THINGS THAT OTHER PEOPLE DO?

MARS OR BUST!

54

A: Because they feel pressured. They want to fit in, be liked, and not be too different. They may be afraid that kids will make fun of them if they don't do what everyone else is doing. Sometimes we assume that a movie, TV show, or product is good because it's popular. We may think, *If so many people do that, it must be fun.* Or, *If so many people have seen that movie, it must be good.* That's OK as long as what's popular is pleasing to God. But no one has to feel pressured to do things that are wrong.

KEY VERSE: *I didn't want to do anything without your consent. And I didn't want you to help because you were forced to do it but because you wanted to. (Philemon 1:14)*

RELATED VERSES: *Matthew 5:19; 1 Corinthians 9:20*

RELATED QUESTION: *What if someone says, "You won't be my friend anymore if you don't do that"? Should you do it?*

NOTE TO PARENTS: *This is a good time in your children's lives to teach them the importance of knowing the difference between right and wrong, having an opinion, and acting on what you believe. Peer pressure will increase dramatically as children get older.*

Q: WHAT SHOULD I DO IF OTHER KIDS LAUGH AT ME FOR GOING TO CHURCH?

55

A: You can ignore their laughter. If you get the chance, you can quietly explain that you go to church because you love God and because you enjoy church and want to be with your family and friends there. Someone who laughs at you for going to church may not know what church is, may have never been to church, and probably doesn't know what it means to love God and his Son, Jesus. That's someone for whom you can pray. You can even invite that person to go to church with you sometime, especially when your church has a fun night or other social activity.

KEY VERSE: *God blesses you who are hated and excluded and mocked and cursed because you are identified with me, the Son of Man. (Luke 6:22)*

RELATED VERSE: *Matthew 5:44*

NOTE TO PARENTS: *Most children don't understand the differences among the various religions and denominations. It's important for them to learn how to accept children from all cultures and backgrounds. They also need to understand, however, that they can't accept all beliefs. Help your children learn what is unique about the Christian faith and about your particular denomination so they will know how to explain what they believe.*

Q: WHY DO YOU HAVE TO BE GOOD AND OBEY IN SCHOOL?

56

A: School leaders and teachers have rules for how students should act in school so that the school will be safe and students will be able to learn. Just think of the confusion if all the kids did whatever they wanted whenever they wanted. No one would learn anything, except how to be rowdy. In class, for example, if everyone talked at the same time, no one would hear the teacher. And if kids were allowed to run, push, and shove in the hall, people would get hurt.

KEY VERSE: *Oh, why didn't I listen to my teachers? Why didn't I pay attention to those who gave me instruction? (Proverbs 5:13)*

RELATED VERSES: *Romans 13:2; Colossians 2:6*

RELATED QUESTION: *Why do you have to obey other adults besides your parents?*

NOTE TO PARENTS: *Sometimes children can become overwhelmed by all the rules in school. They may even fear that they might break some rules by accident. Help them understand that the rules make sense and that most rules are easy to obey. Help your children understand the long-term benefits of applying themselves in school and doing well. Point out that obeying school leaders is one of the ways that we obey God, who has given us these leaders.*

Q: WHY ARE SOME KIDS SO BIG AND OTHER KIDS SO SMALL?

57

A: People come in all different shapes and sizes. Just look at adults. Some professional football players weigh over three hundred pounds, and some professional basketball players are well over seven feet tall! Most people, however, are much lighter and shorter than that. Kids come in different shapes and sizes too. They also grow at different rates. A girl might grow quickly and seem very tall compared to other kids. But in a few years other kids will begin growing and pass her in height. It can be frustrating to be very small or very tall right now, but eventually these things average out. Be patient. Size won't matter so much in the future when everyone has finished growing.

KEY VERSE: *The Lord said to Samuel, "Don't judge by his appearance or height, for I have rejected him. The Lord doesn't make decisions the way you do! People judge by outward appearance, but the Lord looks at a person's thoughts and intentions." (1 Samuel 16:7)*

RELATED VERSES: *Psalm 139:14-16*

NOTE TO PARENTS: *Tell stories about when you were growing up and when you experienced your growth spurt.*

Q: WHAT IF I DON'T LIKE THE MUSIC THAT EVERYONE ELSE LISTENS TO?

58

A: You don't have to enjoy certain music just because others do. It's like with food. What if everyone else liked french fries, but fries made you sick to your stomach? Would you eat french fries? You wouldn't have to. In the same way, you will develop your own taste in music. It may be the same as others, but it doesn't have to be. Of course you should respect others' tastes too. Don't yell at them to "turn off that stupid music" just because you don't like it. Pay attention to the words, though. If you know they aren't pleasing to God, let your friends know you have no interest in listening.

KEY VERSES: *"Just as the mouth tastes good food, the ear tests the words it hears." So let us discern for ourselves what is right; let us learn together what is good. (Job 34:3-4)*

RELATED VERSES: *Romans 14:1-10*

NOTE TO PARENTS: *The fact is, at about nine or ten years of age, kids begin listening to the music styles that their peers seem to like. Beware of criticizing this music just because you don't appreciate it. Your children may interpret your criticisms as a put-down of their friends, not the music. On the other hand, be sure to point out specific problems you have with certain songs and stations (suggestive lyrics, depraved performers, dirty-talking DJs, and so on) and recommend alternatives. This is the ideal time to help your children learn to appreciate a wide variety of music. And remember that you probably can find a Christian artist for almost every music style.*

Q: I FEEL SO STUPID IN SOME SUBJECTS. WHAT CAN I DO?

59

A: Some subjects are difficult to understand at first—not everyone gets everything right away. God made each person different, each with special gifts. It's normal that some subjects will be easier for you than others. But you can still conquer the ones that seem very difficult. In those classes, you can ask the teacher for help. Most teachers encourage their students to ask questions and to ask for help when they need it. Your parents will also be happy to help you. Subjects that are difficult will help you learn to think and to figure things out.

KEY VERSE: *If you need wisdom—if you want to know what God wants you to do—ask him, and he will gladly tell you. (James 1:5)*

RELATED VERSES: *Proverbs 2:1-2; 22:17; 2 Timothy 2:15*

NOTE TO PARENTS: *Keep in mind that just because kids feel a subject is difficult doesn't mean they lack ability in that subject. Help your children understand that learning difficult material takes work. Do not use words such as stupid or dumb—never hint that your children don't have the mental capability to understand difficult subjects. Instead, challenge your children to do their best. Then give whatever help you're able to offer, find a tutor if needed, and look for ways to affirm your children's work.*

Q: WHY DO SOME KIDS SWEAR?

A: Usually kids swear or curse because they are trying to act older or cool. Some kids live in homes where their parents swear a lot, so they hear the words every day. Or they may have seen movies or videos with a lot of swearing. That makes it easy for them to use swearwords when they talk too. Swearing is a very bad habit to get into. In a certain group at school, it may seem as though swearing will make you accepted. But often people think that those who swear a lot are crude and not very smart. Swearing is *not* cool!

KEY VERSE: *Don't use foul or abusive language. Let everything you say be good and helpful, so that your words will be an encouragement to those who hear them. (Ephesians 4:29)*

RELATED VERSE: *Ephesians 5:4*

NOTE TO PARENTS: *Talk with your kids about swearing and why it's bad. Often kids will repeat a word that they have heard without having a clue about its meaning. When that happens at your house, be careful not to overreact. Instead, explain why the word is bad and help your children understand which words are swearwords and which ones aren't. If you have used swearwords yourself, apologize to your children. Ask them to pray with you, asking God to help you stop saying those kinds of words.*

Q: WHAT SHOULD I SAY IF SOMEONE MAKES FUN OF THE BIBLE?

61

A: If a friend makes fun of the Bible, you can politely explain how you feel and ask that person to stop. Your friend may not know how special the Bible is to you. This might give you a good opportunity to explain that the Bible comes from God, who created the whole universe, and it's very important to you. You might be the first one to help this person understand that the message in the Bible is for everyone in the world. If your friend doesn't want to listen, it's best to let it pass and just pray for him or her.

KEY VERSES: *But even if you suffer for doing what is right, God will reward you for it. So don't be afraid and don't worry. Instead, you must worship Christ as Lord of your life. And if you are asked about your Christian hope, always be ready to explain it. (1 Peter 3:14-15)*

RELATED VERSES: *Proverbs 30:5; John 17:17; 2 Timothy 3:16*

NOTE TO PARENTS: *Talk with your family about the significance of the Scriptures. Be sure your children understand that no other book ever has been or ever will be inspired by God the way the Bible is. God shows us in his Word exactly who he is, how much he loves us, and how important it is for us to love him. This would be another ideal time to teach your children how to explain to others what they believe. See* Ready for Life *(Tyndale House Publishers) for devotions that will help you do this.*

BEING COOL

Dealing with the Desire
to Be Popular

Q: HOW DOES SOMEONE BECOME POPULAR?

62

A: The best way to become popular is to be a positive, helpful, nice person—someone that people enjoy being around. If that's the kind of person you are, kids who get to know you will like you for who you are. Eventually, lots of people will get to know you and like you. Whatever you do, however, don't pretend to be someone you aren't just to be liked by others. Be the kind of person God wants you to be, whether you become popular or not. In other words, be like Jesus!

KEY VERSE: *Be kind to each other, tenderhearted, forgiving one another, just as God through Christ has forgiven you. (Ephesians 4:32)*

RELATED VERSES: *Proverbs 10:32; Ephesians 4:29*

RELATED QUESTIONS: *How do you make people like you? Should I do what my friends do to be popular?*

NOTE TO PARENTS: *Most groups of children develop a natural pecking order, with the most popular kids on top. Children are very aware of this order, and most would like to move up the order. Several factors determine this order—height, attractiveness, silliness, etc. Explain that it's nice to be liked, but a person doesn't have to be liked by everybody. Also, don't be afraid to give extra attention at home. This will go a long way in preventing your children from worrying about their position in any pecking order.*

Q: IS IT OK TO BE POPULAR?

63

A: Nothing is wrong with being popular if it's for the right reasons. Some kids are popular because they are kind and caring. Sometimes Christians are very unpopular, however, because they stand for what is right. They have to say things that people don't want to hear and do what is right even though just about everyone else is doing what is wrong. (The prophets in the Bible sure weren't very popular!) It's much more important to have God's approval than to be popular with people.

KEY VERSE: *Obviously, I'm not trying to be a people pleaser! No, I am trying to please God. If I were still trying to please people, I would not be Christ's servant. (Galatians 1:10)*

RELATED VERSES: *John 5:44; 12:42-43; Acts 5:29; Romans 2:13*

NOTE TO PARENTS: *If your children want to become more popular, don't be concerned—that's normal and all right. They may be trying to figure out what to do to gain popularity. As you give advice about how to act at school, help your kids be aware of God's love for them as well as yours. Being assured of this love will help your children want to please God and please you, which will help fulfill their need to be popular.*

Q: DO YOU HAVE TO WEAR MAKEUP OR DRESS COOL TO MAKE PEOPLE LIKE YOU?

64

A: Some advertisements, television shows, magazines, and movies make it seem that way, but it's not true. Attention and popularity based on makeup and clothes don't last very long. People should like you for who you are. It's good to be neat and to *look* nice, but it's more important to *be* nice. People are drawn to others who are gentle and loving.

KEY VERSES: *Don't be concerned about the outward beauty that depends on fancy hairstyles, expensive jewelry, or beautiful clothes. You should be known for the beauty that comes from within, the unfading beauty of a gentle and quiet spirit, which is so precious to God. (1 Peter 3:3-4)*

RELATED VERSES: *Matthew 6:31-33; Luke 12:15; Philippians 4:11-12; 1 Timothy 6:8*

NOTE TO PARENTS: *Although most young children are not very fashion conscious, many of their parents are. Thus children of all ages can be found dressed like the magazine ads. This puts other kids under pressure to get new clothes all the time. Don't get caught in that trap. You can dress your children nicely and in style without spending a bundle on designer clothes. Let your children know that it's all right to wear the latest fashions (as long as they're not too extreme), but it's vital to be the right kind of person in those clothes. Character, not clothes, makes the person.*

Q:

HOW DO YOU GET SOMEONE TO LIKE YOU IF YOU AREN'T AS POPULAR AS EVERYONE ELSE?

BE RIGHT WITH YOU, MAX, MY MAN. JUST NEED TO ORDER A DOUBLE DECAF LATTE, AND TALK TO THE PRESIDENT OF MY FAN CLUB!

65

A: You can't force people to like you or talk them into it. And you shouldn't do whatever they say just so they will be your friends. When you live for Jesus and let the Holy Spirit control your actions, people will like you for who you are. So the idea is to help people get to know the real you. You can be liked, even if you're not voted Most Popular. Outgoing, likable people are often very popular, but you can be likable even if you're quiet. A few good friends who enjoy doing the same things can be just as much fun as a big group of the most popular kids. God made each person special and unique, so we should value all people (ourself included) no matter how popular they are or aren't.

KEY VERSES: *When the Holy Spirit controls our lives, he will produce this kind of fruit in us: love, joy, peace, patience, kindness, goodness, faithfulness, gentleness, and self-control. (Galatians 5:22-23)*

RELATED VERSES: *Luke 22:24-26*

NOTE TO PARENTS: *As kids grow up, they become acquainted with the pecking order in the various groups to which they belong. (See the note with question 66.) Look for groups—church groups, community choirs, and certain sport teams—where the other kids are more likely to accept your children for who they are. Usually the tone for a group is set by a caring adult.*

Q: WHY DO KIDS THINK SOMETHING IS COOL ONE DAY AND STUPID THE NEXT?

66

A: People change, so those kids may just have changed their minds. Think about times when you did the same thing. What was your favorite TV show last year? How about your favorite music group? Your favorites are probably different now. As kids grow up, they outgrow the things they liked a year or even a few months before. Also remember that fads change quickly. Something is "in" one day and "out" the next. That's a good reason for not getting too carried away trying to follow every fad that comes along.

KEY VERSE: *When I was a child, I spoke and thought and reasoned as a child does. But when I grew up, I put away childish things. (1 Corinthians 13:11)*

RELATED VERSE: *1 Peter 1:24*

NOTE TO PARENTS: *Children are susceptible to fads. Discuss the power of advertisements with your children—ads are the source of many fads. Have fun analyzing the advertisers' strategies and talking back to the TV together when one of those ads comes on. You can say, "Come on, I don't need that!" "Who are you trying to fool?" "No one will want one of those next month!"*

Q: WHY DO SOME KIDS ALL DRESS, TALK, AND ACT THE SAME?

67

A: People like to belong, to be accepted as part of a group. Many times kids will cluster into groups of friends, almost like a club. Then those kids will dress alike, talk alike, and act alike. Maybe they're afraid of being singled out or laughed at, or maybe they're all together because they just like the same things. It's all right to be part of a group, but be careful not to become a clique (a group that thinks it's too good for anyone else). And don't allow any group to convince you to dress, talk, and act in a way you don't want to or that you know is wrong. Be committed to what you believe, and be confident about your own tastes.

KEY VERSES: *If you love only those who love you, what good is that? Even corrupt tax collectors do that much. If you are kind only to your friends, how are you different from anyone else? Even pagans do that. (Matthew 5:46-47)*

RELATED VERSE: *1 John 2:15*

RELATED QUESTION: *If I want to join a group of kids, should I be like them?*

NOTE TO PARENTS: *Fitting in with peers can be a big deal to children. Try to accommodate your kids without going overboard. Let them know that it's all right to be like everyone else in a group as long as what they do doesn't keep them from pleasing God. Then encourage them to stay friends with others who aren't part of their group.*

Q: SHOULD I GET A COOL NICKNAME?

68

A: Nicknames are fun to have, especially if they make us sound good. But nicknames often come from others—the names describe how other people see us. It's not the same if we give them to ourselves. You don't need to have a good nickname to be a good person. If your friends give you a nickname that you like, however, let them know that it's OK for them to keep calling you by that name.

KEY VERSES: *These are the names of the twelve [Jesus] chose: Simon (he renamed him Peter), James and John (the sons of Zebedee, but Jesus nicknamed them "Sons of Thunder"). (Mark 3:16-17)*

RELATED VERSE: *Acts 4:36*

NOTE TO PARENTS: *Unfortunately, kids can pin cruel or demeaning nicknames on their peers, so don't give your children's peers any ammunition by using unusual nicknames with your children in public. If you have a pet name or nickname for your child held over from earlier years ("precious," "bunny," "babycakes," "champ," and so on), make sure it won't turn out to be used in a derogatory way outside your home.*

Q: DO YOU HAVE TO BE GOOD AT A SPORT TO BE POPULAR?

69

A: Good athletes are often popular because people enjoy sports and like winners. But all athletes aren't well liked, and you don't have to be athletic to be popular. Don't try to be something you're not. If you're in a sport, do your best and play hard and fair—enjoy yourself instead of worrying about what others think. If you're not good at sports, most likely you enjoy other kinds of activities. Be yourself, and let popularity take care of itself.

KEY VERSE: *Physical exercise has some value, but spiritual exercise is much more important, for it promises a reward in both this life and the next. (1 Timothy 4:8)*

RELATED VERSE: *1 Corinthians 9:25*

RELATED QUESTION: *Why are heroes so popular?*

NOTE TO PARENTS: *Your children may suddenly become interested in sports or want to join a team because they want to be popular. Often kids will want to try a sport because other friends are playing. You may think that your children are doing it for the wrong reasons. That's all right. It may be a way to broaden their interests and skills. Sports will also help them develop social skills, such as teamwork.*

Q: IF SOMEONE ISN'T POPULAR, HOW COME OTHERS THINK LESS OF HIM OR HER AS A PERSON?

GET MUSCLE
BUILDER'S
AUTOGRAPH

ACME BODY PADDING

70

A: Popular kids aren't better than others just because of their popularity, especially if they are popular for the wrong reasons. Each person, including you, is a valuable creation of God. Looking down on others is never right, for the Bible teaches that all people are important to God and valuable in his sight. God wants us to treat everyone well and with respect. If you're wondering why more popular kids don't pay more attention to you, be careful that you aren't busy ignoring other kids who seem even less popular. Go out of your way to make others feel good and respected, no matter how popular they are.

KEY VERSES: *Then these righteous ones will reply, "Lord, when did we ever see you hungry and feed you? Or thirsty and give you something to drink? Or a stranger and show you hospitality? Or naked and give you clothing? When did we ever see you sick or in prison, and visit you?" And the King will tell them, "I assure you, when you did it to one of the least of these my brothers and sisters, you were doing it to me!" (Matthew 25:37-40)*

RELATED VERSES: *Psalm 100:3; 139:14; John 5:41; 1 Corinthians 4:3-4, 10-13; Ephesians 2:10*

NOTE TO PARENTS: *The real problem may be that your children believe that others think less of them. They may be experiencing rejection. When the social-life road at school becomes bumpy, the atmosphere at home becomes especially important. Spend one-on-one time with your children, for they may be the "brothers and sisters" for whom Jesus wants you to do things right now.*

Q: WHY DOES MY FRIEND ALWAYS WANT ME TO ASK PEOPLE WHAT THEY THINK ABOUT HER?

71

A: Your friend may be unsure and afraid. She may think that no one likes her, and perhaps she is afraid to talk directly to people. Try not to get caught in a situation like this. Instead, assure your friend that *you* like her—*you* think she's special. If you would like to help her get to know more people, invite her to a group activity at your church. Or invite another friend or two over to your house when you invite her. If your friend wants you to ask boys whether or not they like her, it's better not to get involved.

KEY VERSE: *Encourage each other. Live in harmony and peace. Then the God of love and peace will be with you. (2 Corinthians 13:11)*

RELATED VERSES: *1 Samuel 20:3-17; 1 Thessalonians 5:14*

RELATED QUESTION: *Should you ask people what they think about you?*

NOTE TO PARENTS: *As kids get older, it's natural for them to begin feeling concerned with what others think about them. Help your children learn to affirm their friends, to make their friends feel good about themselves. Make your home a safe place where the friends feel welcomed and accepted.*

Q: SHOULD I HANG OUT WITH POPULAR PEOPLE TO BECOME POPULAR?

72

A: This may seem like the way to be popular, but that kind of popularity is pretty shallow and won't last very long. It's OK to be friends with the popular kids, but it's not OK to do whatever they say to be accepted by them. Instead, be the right kind of person, the kind that others will want to hang with. Be confident in the fact that God loves you. Remember that the Bible teaches us to think about the needs of others, not just our own. Spend some time and attention on kids who aren't very popular and help them feel good about themselves. You'll be amazed at how good *you* will feel when you make others feel good.

KEY VERSE: *Oh, that my actions would consistently reflect your principles! (Psalm 119:5)*

RELATED VERSES: *Proverbs 13:20; 1 John 3:18-19*

RELATED QUESTION: *If the popular kids won't let me hang out with them, should I ask why not?*

NOTE TO PARENTS: *Physical, mental, and social maturity varies greatly among children. In addition, some kids within a grade can be as much as eleven months older than the others. If your children are less mature, they may want to hang around with more mature kids to become more popular. But this probably is not a good idea. Get to know your children's friends so you can determine the kind of influence these friends have on your children. Encourage friendships with kids at similar stages of development by offering to have them over even before your children ask.*

MAKING THE GRADE

Relating to Teachers

Q: WHY IS IT THAT SOME TEACHERS ARE NICE TO OTHER KIDS BUT MEAN TO ME?

73

A: Most teachers try to be fair and treat all their students the same. But here are three situations that can make it seem otherwise:

1. It's easy to be nice to students who listen carefully, try to learn, do their assignments on time, and stay out of trouble. And it's natural to *not* be attracted to kids who seem to have bad attitudes.

2. God gave people different personalities. Thus, although we should love everyone, we get along better with some than others. This is also true with teachers. You'll find that you will get along OK with some teachers and great with others.

3. Some kids get nervous wondering how a teacher feels about them. Therefore, they misinterpret some of the teacher's words or actions as being negative toward them.

If you have problems with a certain teacher, pray about it; then do your best to cooperate and learn. That combination often works wonders.

KEY VERSES: *My child, never forget the things I have taught you. Store my commands in your heart. Then you will find favor with both God and people, and you will gain a good reputation. (Proverbs 3:1, 4)*

RELATED VERSE: *Luke 6:31*

RELATED QUESTIONS: *Why are some teachers tough? Why are some teachers mean but others nice?*

NOTE TO PARENTS: *If your child complains that a teacher is mean, don't judge the teacher. Instead, talk it through with your child to see if together you can figure out the situation. If that doesn't work, talk to the teacher and get the other side of the story.*

WHY DO SOME TEACHERS LET YOU GET AWAY WITH STUFF WHILE OTHERS GIVE YOU TROUBLE WHEN YOU DROP A PENCIL?

74

A: Some teachers are pretty relaxed, and others are more nervous and on edge. Some teachers have few rules in class, while others are more strict. One way is not better than the other. If your teacher is kind of nervous and strict, then be careful to act right and obey the rules. You can get along with any teacher if you try. Remember that even after you grow up, you'll always have to relate to different types of people. For example, you may have a boss who is strict. If you can get along with others, you'll have more opportunities to advance and succeed. If you can't, you may become frustrated and discouraged.

KEY VERSE: *A student is not greater than the teacher. A servant is not greater than the master. (Matthew 10:24)*

RELATED VERSE: *Romans 13:3*

RELATED QUESTION: *Why do some kids get all the attention and some just get into trouble?*

NOTE TO PARENTS: *Teachers who seem strict and keep their class under control are often more systematic and organized with their teaching methods. Kids who tend to be creative or people-oriented may complain about this type of teacher. But those types of students may benefit the most from this approach. Help your children understand that a strict teacher isn't necessarily mean—class discipline is more complicated than that.*

WHY DO TEACHERS MAKE IT EASY FOR SOME KIDS TO GET GOOD GRADES AND HARD FOR OTHERS?

75

A: It may seem as though teachers sometimes make it easier for some kids than others, but all teachers try to be fair. They really try to treat everyone the same. Also, most teachers are more concerned that their students try hard and do their best. They want kids to learn, not just get good grades. So they might push some students to work harder. Instead of worrying about others, make sure that *you* work hard and do *your* best.

KEY VERSE: *Brothers and sisters, we urge you to warn those who are lazy. Encourage those who are timid. Take tender care of those who are weak. Be patient with everyone. (1 Thessalonians 5:14)*

RELATED VERSE: *Ezekiel 33:20*

RELATED QUESTIONS: *Why do we have to have tests? Why do teachers have to grade tests? What's the point of a teacher drawing a happy face on your test?*

NOTE TO PARENTS: *Teachers may push kids who they believe are not working up to their potential. In other words, one student may work hard just to understand the material and pass the class, while another may be coasting to an A. The teacher may push the A student harder to challenge that child. Let your children know that the teacher may be tougher on them because they are able to learn even more than they have been learning.*

Q: WHY DO TEACHERS GIVE SO MUCH HOMEWORK?

76

A: Teachers give homework because they are trying to be *good* teachers and they want to help you learn. Doing assignments at home will remind you of what the teacher said in class and help you put it into practice. The school system was designed to include homework. It's not a punishment—homework is an important part of learning.

The best way to get the homework done is to start on it right away. Don't put off doing an assignment until the last minute. It's a good idea to do homework *first,* before watching TV, playing with friends, or talking on the phone. Even when you don't have assignments to do at home, you can review what you learned that day with your family.

KEY VERSE: *If you stop listening to instruction, my child, you have turned your back on knowledge. (Proverbs 19:27)*

RELATED VERSES: *Proverbs 17:16; 21:5; 2 Timothy 2:15*

RELATED QUESTIONS: *Why do we never get homework on Fridays? Why do we have to do homework?*

NOTE TO PARENTS: *Homework can be a blessing if it helps kids learn organizational skills and discipline. Help your children develop a daily schedule, and encourage them to do the work without your nagging. Too much homework may pile up on one night, especially if the schedule is already jammed. For example, one afternoon and evening schedule might include a music lesson, sports practice, and a Bible club meeting. When that happens, you will have to set priorities. Teachers, coaches, and church leaders will usually understand and work with you if you talk to them about your dilemma.*

Q: WHY WON'T THE TEACHER LET ME SIT NEXT TO MY FRIEND?

77

A: Your teacher probably knows that you won't learn very much if you're seated next to your friend. Sometimes when friends sit next to each other, they talk or pass notes instead of paying attention. The purpose of school is to learn, and teachers want their students to learn without distractions. You can still play with your friends at recess or sit with them at lunch.

If you do get an opportunity to sit next to a friend, pay attention and don't talk or goof around. When your teacher sees that you and your friend are paying attention and learning, then there won't be any reason to separate the two of you.

KEY VERSE: *Work brings profit, but mere talk leads to poverty! (Proverbs 14:23)*

RELATED VERSE: *Proverbs 23:12*

NOTE TO PARENTS: *Help your kids understand that it's good to have friends, and you are glad that they have friends at school, but learning comes first. Explain to your children the importance of obeying the rules and not distracting others, no matter whom they are sitting beside. Who knows, they might end up sitting next to a friend someday!*

Q: WHY DO WE HAVE TO RESPECT TEACHERS?

78

A: The Bible says that God expects his people to respect those in authority over them. That includes teachers. Also, for teachers to do their best, they need the respect of their students. If you respect your teachers, you'll be polite and kind to them, listen to them, and do what they say. Remember, the only one who benefits from your going to school and learning is you. If you don't cooperate, listen, and learn, you won't be hurting the teacher—you will be hurting yourself and your future.

KEY VERSE: *For the authorities do not frighten people who are doing right, but they frighten those who do wrong. So do what they say, and you will get along well. (Romans 13:3)*

RELATED VERSE: *Luke 6:40*

RELATED QUESTIONS: *Why don't some students respect teachers? If teachers want us to respect and obey them, they will first have to respect us as children. Right?*

NOTE TO PARENTS: *You may not always agree with your children's teachers, but let your kids know that you still respect these people. Teach your children that when you send them to school, you are extending your parental authority over them to their teachers and school administrators. So if they are disrespectful or disobedient to the school authorities, they are doing the same to you.*

Q: WHY ARE SOME CHILDREN SUSPENDED FROM SCHOOL?

79

A: The purpose of school is to provide a safe environment where students learn the things they need to know as they grow up. Children who break rules related to weapons, drugs, fighting, and so on, make it difficult for everyone else in the class to learn. Sometimes those kids have to be taken out of the classroom or even be suspended from school for everyone else's good. Hopefully their punishment will teach them not to threaten the safety of their classmates.

KEY VERSE: *Throw out the mocker, and fighting, quarrels, and insults will disappear. (Proverbs 22:10)*

RELATED VERSES: *Proverbs 19:25; 21:11*

NOTE TO PARENTS: *Just a few years ago, suspension was very rare in elementary schools. Recently, however, because of the violence among younger children, every threat is taken seriously, and children are being suspended for saying things like "I'll kill you" or "I'll get you." Help your children understand that a suspension is very serious. Kids who have been suspended from school may have done something more serious than the rest of the class realizes.*

Q: WHY DO KIDS OFTEN TAKE ADVANTAGE OF A SUBSTITUTE TEACHER?

80

A: Students think the substitute doesn't know them, the class procedures and rules, or what the kids have been studying. So some students think they can get away with things like being rude or not doing what the substitute says. If other kids ask you to join them in tricking the substitute, don't go along with them. Substitute teachers should be treated with respect, just the same as regular teachers. Besides, the substitute will probably leave a note for the regular teacher that tells how everyone acted in class!

KEY VERSE: *Give to everyone what you owe them . . . and give respect and honor to all to whom it is due. (Romans 13:7)*

RELATED VERSES: *1 Corinthians 16:10; 1 Peter 2:17*

RELATED QUESTION: *When our class gets a substitute teacher, why do we say that our teacher lets us out fifteen minutes early?*

NOTE TO PARENTS: *Even though giving a substitute teacher a hard time seems to be a time-honored tradition, we should let our children know that we expect them not to get involved.*

WHY DON'T TEACHERS JUST GET TO THE POINT INSTEAD OF BLABBING ON AND ON ABOUT THE SUBJECT?

81

A: Some kids find it more difficult to learn certain subjects than other kids. Good teachers take time to teach *all* the students in a class, not just the ones who understand the material right away. Sometimes teachers explain other material that is also important, adding facts and reasons for what they are teaching. Listen and pay attention—you may learn something!

KEY VERSE: *[The Levites] read from the Book of the Law of God and clearly explained the meaning of what was being read, helping the people understand each passage. (Nehemiah 8:8)*

RELATED VERSES: *Joshua 8:34-35; Ecclesiastes 12:11; Philippians 3:1*

RELATED QUESTIONS: *Why do teachers explain things too much? Why can't teachers give you a sheet to tell you what to do? Why do teachers get mad at you for not understanding if they didn't explain very well?*

NOTE TO PARENTS: *In elementary school, teachers usually do not give long lectures. If your children ask this question, the problem may be that they do not feel challenged in class. Or it may be that one of your children has a learning disability or a different learning style and has difficulty understanding what is being taught. You may want to talk with the teacher about this. You could explain that you think your child might respond better to written instructions than to oral ones.*

Q: WHY DO MY FRIENDS GET FUN TEACHERS AND I GET MEAN ONES?

82

A: Let's face it, some teachers are more fun than others. Everyone is different, and it takes all kinds of teachers to teach all kinds of kids. But no one is trying to make sure that you don't get any fun teachers. Take a good attitude to class and give your teachers a chance. You may find that they are more fun than you thought. Also, remember the "grass is greener" syndrome—other kids may think that *you* have the fun teachers.

KEY VERSE: *Indeed, the Teacher taught the plain truth, and he did so in an interesting way. (Ecclesiastes 12:10)*

RELATED QUESTION: *Why don't teachers just let us play all day?*

NOTE TO PARENTS: *Encourage your children to have a good attitude toward their teachers. Teachers who seem mean may just be trying to establish their authority in the classroom at the beginning of the year. A few weeks later, those teachers may loosen up if the class is under control.*

WHY DOESN'T THE TEACHER EVER CHOOSE MY PAPERS OR PICTURES TO PUT ON THE WALL?

83

A: Teachers usually choose very good papers to display in class. *Very good* may mean the highest score on a test or homework. *Very good* may be a beautiful picture or project. But *very good* can also mean showing great improvement. The teacher may want to recognize a student who has made great progress in the class. Do your best. It's an honor to have your work displayed, but don't worry about it. Just because your paper didn't go on the wall doesn't mean it's not good. Doing your best is more important than having a paper displayed.

KEY VERSE: *Be sure to do what you should, for then you will enjoy the personal satisfaction of having done your work well, and you won't need to compare yourself to anyone else. (Galatians 6:4)*

RELATED VERSE: *Romans 12:15*

NOTE TO PARENTS: *Look for ways to affirm your children's work. Display their tests, homework assignments, and artwork on your refrigerator or wall, complimenting them for doing their best.*

Q: WHY DO SOME TEACHERS HAVE RULES THAT DON'T EVEN MAKE SENSE?

TEACHER, TEACHER! WHY AREN'T WE ALLOWED TO ASK QUESTIONS DURING CLASS?

84

A: Almost all rules have good reasons behind them. Sometimes, however, the reasons may not be obvious, so those rules may not make sense to you. It's all right to ask a teacher for the reasons, but be sure to ask nicely. It's important to have a good attitude in class. You should obey all rules whether you like them or not. If all the kids disobeyed the rules or just obeyed the rules they liked, no one would be able to learn anything.

KEY VERSE: *Help me understand the meaning of your commandments. (Psalm 119:27)*

RELATED VERSE: *Proverbs 6:23*

RELATED QUESTIONS: *Why aren't we allowed to chew gum in class? Why do we have recess for just half an hour instead of an hour?*

NOTE TO PARENTS: *Encourage and compliment your children for wanting to know the reasons behind rules. Let them know it's all right to ask questions like that. Be sure, however, that they really want answers and aren't just looking for an excuse to break a rule. When children understand the reason behind a rule and how people benefit from it, most of them usually have no problem following it.*

SUBJECT MATTERS

Succeeding in Class

WHY DO WE HAVE TO STUDY SUBJECTS THAT WE MIGHT NOT NEED TO KNOW WHEN WE GROW UP?

85

A: People may think that the only reason to study a subject in school is to learn something that they might need in a future job. But that's wrong. Some classes teach information and skills that students can build on. Some classes teach students how to think. Most of what you learn in the early grades of school, such as reading and math, will help you in many areas of your life. Also, you never know when God will use you and what you have learned to help others. It will be exciting to see how God will someday use what you're learning now.

KEY VERSE: *Teach the wise, and they will be wiser. Teach the righteous, and they will learn more. (Proverbs 9:9)*

RELATED VERSES: *Proverbs 27:1; Daniel 1:4; 2 Timothy 3:17*

RELATED QUESTIONS: *Why do we have to study? If kids don't like subjects, why don't teachers make them more fun?*

NOTE TO PARENTS: *Encourage your children to try to do well in all their subjects. Help them understand that the things they learn now will prepare them for many things, not just for a future job. For example, they may need to know how to follow recipes, teach Sunday school, plant a garden, etc. Because no one knows the future, no one can predict which subjects will or won't be of value.*

IF YOU HAVE ALREADY STUDIED SOMETHING, SUCH AS ADDITION, WHY DO YOU HAVE TO KEEP STUDYING IT?

86

A: To get really good at anything, a person has to practice. This can mean doing the same drills, playing the same scales, or reviewing the same material over and over. It's true in sports and music, and it's true in math and other subjects. Also, the simple problems will lead to more complicated ones. You won't be able to move on to the more difficult problems if you haven't mastered the easy ones.

KEY VERSES: *Then you will understand what is right, just, and fair, and you will know how to find the right course of action every time. For wisdom will enter your heart, and knowledge will fill you with joy. (Proverbs 2:9-10)*

RELATED VERSE: *Philippians 3:1*

RELATED QUESTION: *When my math is easy, why don't they give me hard math?*

NOTE TO PARENTS: *Textbooks and the curriculum of a school district are designed to review and reinforce previous learning. Usually the first part of each school year is spent reviewing facts and skills learned the year before. This may be boring for some children, but help yours to understand that it is necessary.*

Q: WHY DO SOME PEOPLE FIND A SUBJECT HARD, AND OTHERS FIND IT EASY?

87

A: Some people do better in math. Others do better in reading and writing. Still others do better because they work harder than most students. They listen in class, ask questions, and do their homework. Some people may learn a certain subject right away because God gave them the ability to do so. People are good at different things. Isn't that great?

KEY VERSE: *God gave [Daniel, Shadrach, Meshach, and Abednego] an unusual aptitude for learning the literature and science of the time. And God gave Daniel special ability in understanding the meanings of visions and dreams. (Daniel 1:17)*

RELATED VERSES: *Proverbs 14:6; James 1:5*

NOTE TO PARENTS: *Explain to your children that just about everyone has to work hard at some subjects. It may be because of something as simple as life experience. For example, a kid who has moved often and has traveled a lot may know geography better than those who have lived in the same place all their lives.*

Q: WHY IS IT SO HARD TO FIND THINGS IN MY DESK?

88

A: Probably because it's jammed with a lot of stuff. It's a good idea to go through your desk and take out all the notes, wrappers, old papers, stale food, broken pencils, and other extra materials that you don't need for your classes. Next, make sure that everything you do need is in there. Then organize everything; that is, put each item in a certain place so you know where it is and can find it when you need it. Try straightening out your desk at the beginning or end of each day. That will keep you from filling it with junk.

KEY VERSE: *Commit your work to the Lord, and then your plans will succeed. (Proverbs 16:3)*

NOTE TO PARENTS: *Make sure your children don't have such cluttered desks that they lose assignments, teacher notes, tests, permission forms, etc. If this is a problem for any of the kids in your family, talk with the teacher and design a course of action together.*

Q: HOW CAN I STOP DAYDREAMING AND PAY BETTER ATTENTION IN CLASS?

89

A: It's easy to let your mind wander and daydream in class, especially when you don't find the subject very interesting. One way to concentrate and stop daydreaming is to take notes about what the teacher is saying, maybe even write down questions that come to mind. If this doesn't work, ask your teacher for suggestions about what you can do. Teachers like it when their students *want* to learn, and they will be happy to help.

KEY VERSE: *Commit everything you do to the Lord. Trust him, and he will help you. (Psalm 37:5)*

RELATED VERSES: *Proverbs 2:1-4*

NOTE TO PARENTS: *Some children struggle with this. It's difficult for them to stop daydreaming once they've started. If you think this is a problem for any of your children, you may want to schedule a teacher conference. If your kids know that the teacher will ask them at least one question at the end of each class, they may be motivated to break the habit.*

Q:

DO YOU NEED TO LEARN MATH ONLY IF YOU WANT TO BE A PILOT OR A CONSTRUCTION WORKER?

90

A: You'd be surprised how math is used in life. People in all kinds of jobs use math every day, not just pilots and construction workers. Engineers, writers, homemakers, musicians, doctors, managers, and even professional athletes use math. Go figure. Even if you just wanted to paint a room in your house, you'd use math to figure out how much paint to buy. Almost everything you learn now will help you understand the things you need to know later, whatever you end up doing.

KEY VERSE: *Intelligent people are always open to new ideas. In fact, they look for them. (Proverbs 18:15)*

RELATED VERSES: *Ecclesiastes 7:11-12*

NOTE TO PARENTS: *You can have fun with this by discussing a variety of occupations and showing how each one uses math. Explain how math is important on your job and in the rest of your life. For example, explain what you do when you balance your checkbook. (In addition, you can show how to divide the responsibilities at home by multiplying the factors involved in making your decisions!)*

Q: WHY DO WE HAVE TO LEARN GEOGRAPHY AND HISTORY?

91

A: Geography helps you learn about the world and gives you information about your own country as well as other countries and their citizens. People travel more than ever these days. One day you might be able to visit some of the countries that you have studied. Wouldn't *that* be exciting! Because of the Internet, TV, and other communication tools, people all over the world seem closer. History is an important subject too. It teaches lessons from the past that we need to learn so we won't repeat the same mistakes that people made before.

KEY VERSE: *All these events happened to them as examples for us. They were written down to warn us, who live at the time when this age is drawing to a close. (1 Corinthians 10:11)*

RELATED VERSES: *Deuteronomy 4:9; Psalm 106:7-8*

RELATED QUESTION: *What's the point of history?*

NOTE TO PARENTS: *One way to help your children see how these subjects are relevant is to talk about your ancestors, where they lived, and what was going on in the world in their time. Also, you might tell about a subject you didn't like when you were a kid, but which turned out to be important in your life.*

Q: WHY ARE GRADES SO IMPORTANT?

92

A: Tests and grades help teachers check to see what students have learned. Grades also help students and their parents see how well the kids are doing at school. Use your grades as a tool to help you see where you need to work harder. Remember that grades don't make a person better or worse than anyone else. More important than grades is whether you're doing your best and learning the material.

KEY VERSE: *Work hard so God can approve you. Be a good worker, one who does not need to be ashamed and who correctly explains the word of truth. (2 Timothy 2:15).*

RELATED QUESTIONS: *Do I need good grades? What's the difference between an A and a D? Shouldn't you always try your best, even in tough spots in life?*

NOTE TO PARENTS: *Some children need to be constantly held accountable for their grades, and they need encouragement to work harder. Other children get straight A's without even trying—these kids may need to be pushed to do extra work. Still other students may be obsessed with getting good grades and be devastated with a B. They might need encouragement to relax about the letter grade. Whatever categories your children fall into, make it clear to them that grades are a tool, not a goal.*

Q: WHY DO PEOPLE CHEAT?

93

A: People cheat because they're lazy. They don't want to work hard to complete an assignment or do well on a test. Cheating is wrong because it's lying, and God tells us not to lie. People cheat in many areas, not just school. Some cheat in games—trying to win without following the rules. Some cheat with money, and others cheat by not being honest with their friends. People who fall into a pattern of cheating find it hard to stop. Kids who cheat in school keep themselves from learning. Then they have to cheat again. After a while, people who cheat lose confidence in themselves and their ability to learn anything. Don't be a cheater—you will cheat yourself.

KEY VERSE: *Unless you are faithful in small matters, you won't be faithful in large ones. If you cheat even a little, you won't be honest with greater responsibilities. (Luke 16:10)*

RELATED VERSES: *Proverbs 11:1; 20:23*

RELATED QUESTIONS: *Can't you just look at one answer on a test? Why do some people cheat on tests and never get caught? Why can't I help my best friend with his math test?*

NOTE TO PARENTS: *It's easy for kids to get into the habit of cheating. If your children have been caught cheating, don't let them try to explain it away. And don't overlook an incident, rationalizing that it was a onetime occurrence. Also, don't think that one talk will solve the problem. Allow your children to experience punishment for cheating. Then return to the issue several times over the ensuing months until you are sure that they have learned their lesson and are determined to stop cheating.*

Q: HOW CAN I DO BETTER IN SPELLING?

94

A: The way to improve in any subject is to study and practice. You can become a better speller by reviewing the assigned words many times. Get someone to help you by testing you on those words. Your parents will be happy to help. Reading more will also help you improve your spelling because you will see words spelled correctly in the books. If you are writing with a computer and using spell-checker, stop and review the actual spelling when corrected. Ask your parents to look over your papers before you turn them in. If you keep working on this every time you write something, you will improve.

KEY VERSE: *Plans go wrong for lack of advice; many counselors bring success. (Proverbs 15:22)*

NOTE TO PARENTS: *Don't berate your children about the difficulties of spelling. Some children learn to spell more easily than others. Kids need to develop a working command of the language, but it should be fun for them. Take time to review spelling words with your children, and help them find a review method that works for them.*

Q: THE KIDS AROUND ME KEEP GETTING ME INTO TROUBLE. WHAT CAN I DO?

95

A: First, you can ignore the other kids. If you don't give them your attention, they probably will stop trying to get you to do what is wrong. If this doesn't work, ask the teacher to change your seat. To do your best in class, you need to be quiet and listen carefully to the teacher. Remember, no one can *make* you do something wrong or break the rules. Other kids can *pressure* you, but in the end *you* always make the decision. Decide that no matter what the kids around you do or how much they pressure you, you will do what is right. And you will do your best to focus on studying your lessons.

KEY VERSE: *Stay away from fools, for you won't find knowledge there. (Proverbs 14:7)*

RELATED VERSE: *Psalm 35:11*

NOTE TO PARENTS: *The first challenge is to see if the trouble is being started by the other kids or by your child. Don't be afraid to ask the teacher to move your child to a different seat, no matter who is initiating the trouble. Help your child understand that the they-made-me-do-it excuse isn't valid. Children need to learn that they are responsible for their actions and that their parents will hold them to that responsibility. This knowledge will motivate them to stand their ground.*

Q: I WANT TO GET A'S, BUT MY FRIENDS SAY GETTING GOOD GRADES IS DUMB. WHAT SHOULD I DO?

96

A: It's always important to do what is right and to do your best no matter what others think or say. Some kids make fun of getting good grades because they don't want to work hard to get those grades. Others may think that it's not cool to seem smart. They're wrong. It's really cool to do well in school. Doing well now will lead to doing well in high school and college, which will lead to doing well in adult life. Kids who think that it's not cool to get good marks may think that they are somehow cheating the system, but they are only cheating themselves.

KEY VERSE: *It is senseless to pay tuition to educate a fool who has no heart for wisdom. (Proverbs 17:16)*

RELATED VERSES: *Proverbs 1:20-23; 9:12*

NOTE TO PARENTS: *This issue can be a problem for gifted students. Often, they get bad grades on purpose because they fear rejection from their peers. Parental support and friendship with other children who are interested in doing well in school can help to solve this problem. Sometimes peer groups will place a high value on doing poorly in school. This is why parental involvement is very important. Let your children know that you expect them to do their best, regardless of what others think or say. Of course your children don't have to broadcast or brag about their grades—encourage them not to do either of those things.*

Q: WHEN KIDS MISS A LOT OF SCHOOL, HOW DO THEY PASS?

97

A: Anyone who misses a lot of school will have a tough time catching up on the work. Kids who are ill or out of town on a trip sometimes get help from a tutor. When there is a good reason for missing school, teachers will give parents the assignments. Then the kids can do their work at home and try to keep up with the class. Parents can also help by teaching their children themselves.

KEY VERSE: *Learn to be wise, and develop good judgment. (Proverbs 4:5)*

NOTE TO PARENTS: *If this subject comes up, explain that just because kids are away from school doesn't mean that they aren't doing any schoolwork.*

Q: WHY DO WE HAVE TO STUDY COMPUTERS?

98

A: Computers are becoming a very important part of society, and they are getting easier and easier to use. Almost every kind of store and business uses computers—from grocery stores to car-repair shops. By using computers people can keep on learning more and more about almost everything there is to know. So studying computers will become more and more important. There is no doubt that computers will be part of everyone's adult life. People who know how to use computers will get good jobs and will be able to help others.

KEY VERSE: *Wise people treasure knowledge, but the babbling of a fool invites trouble. (Proverbs 10:14)*

RELATED VERSES: *Proverbs 15:14; 18:15*

RELATED QUESTIONS: *Why do people need to type? Why do we never play computer games? Why do we hardly ever get to use the computer, and then only for a little bit of time?*

NOTE TO PARENTS: *Most schools don't have enough computers for all kids to get enough practice on them. Your children might want more access, or you might want this for them. If you don't have a computer at home, let your child use one at the public library.*

SAVED BY THE BELL

Choosing Activities

Q: WHY DO SOME PEOPLE THINK THE INTERNET IS BAD?

99

A: The Internet has countless Web pages of all kinds, and it is expanding every day. The Internet can be a wonderful tool for finding facts and learning more about everything. Unfortunately, not all the information on the Internet is good. Some people tell lies on the Internet, and some Web sites have terrible pictures. When people read about these bad things, some of them think that the Internet is all bad. It's a tool, however, like a knife. Knives have many good uses, such as cutting and carving. But they can also be used for evil. The same can be said about television. It can be entertaining and provide helpful information, but it can also promote bad values and actions. Like all tools, the Internet can be used for good or evil. Make sure that you use it for good.

***

KEY VERSE: *Whatever you eat or drink or whatever you do, you must do all for the glory of God. (1 Corinthians 10:31)*

NOTE TO PARENTS: *Help your children know that the Internet can provide good adventures and dangerous ones. If you have a computer at home with Internet access, be sure to monitor your children's use of it, just as you do with television.*

Q: WHY DON'T I HAVE ENOUGH TIME TO PLAY?

A: Schedules get packed with activities, lessons, sports, and schoolwork. Sometimes it seems as if there's no time to play. If this is a problem for you, talk with your parents about it. After you have done your homework and activities, there should be some time to play. If your schedule is too full, you and your family can talk about the possibility of eliminating some activities.

KEY VERSE: *There is a time for everything, a season for every activity under heaven. (Ecclesiastes 3:1)*

NOTE TO PARENTS: *These days, kids are busier than ever. When teachers give too much homework, coaches call too many practices, and parents want their children involved in too many activities, time for play may get squeezed out. But play is an important creative outlet for children and a good way for them to reduce their stress. Be careful not to make your children's schedules too full. And remember that play is important for adults too—try to schedule time each week to relax and play as a family.*

Q: WHY DON'T WE HAVE GYM CLASS EVERY DAY?

101

A: Each school has its own schedule. The schedule depends on many factors: the number of students, the classes that students are required to take, the number of teachers, the rooms available, etc. It would be fun to have gym every day, but that might not be possible in your school. After school or on weekends you may want to be part of a sports team, take swimming lessons, or do something else you enjoy. You can do these things with friends or family.

KEY VERSE: *Physical exercise has some value, but spiritual exercise is much more important, for it promises a reward in both this life and the next. (1 Timothy 4:8)*

NOTE TO PARENTS: *This question may come from the fact that kids are full of energy and need a physical outlet. Organized sports and playing with friends can meet that need.*

Q:

WHEN YOU ARE HOME DURING THE SUMMER AND NOBODY IS AROUND, WHAT CAN YOU DO TO HAVE SOME FUN?

102

A: Use your imagination. You could plant a garden, collect rocks or insects, take pictures, or check out the neighborhood to find some new friends. You could go to the library to read magazines and books or use the computers. You could organize a garage sale. You could ask your parents how you might help around the house. Perhaps these suggestions will help you think of other fun ways to keep busy during the summer.

KEY VERSE: *So I recommend having fun, because there is nothing better for people to do in this world than to eat, drink, and enjoy life. That way they will experience some happiness along with all the hard work God gives them. (Ecclesiastes 8:15)*

RELATED QUESTION: *What are some good things to do when you're not in school?*

NOTE TO PARENTS: *When kids seem bored, some parents merely tell them to find something to do and may say something like "Only boring people get bored." It's better to make specific suggestions and to offer help in finding something fun to do around the house. Help your children think of ideas themselves, by asking them questions and showing them how to go through a mental list of options.*

103

A: Your parents probably have a good reason for wanting you to play soccer. They may want you to learn teamwork and good sportsmanship and to stay in good physical condition. So give the sport a chance. If you still don't like soccer after playing for a while, talk it over with your parents. Be respectful and explain how you feel. Suggest other ways to have the same kind of experience—like playing another sport or being in a club that you would enjoy more. It's good to learn a wide variety of skills. Soccer or something else you are learning may not be your favorite, but if you try hard anyway and see it through to the end of the season, you will learn lessons and gain another skill that you may use in the future. Your parents are more likely to grant your request for a change if they know you gave it 100 percent.

KEY VERSES: *Children, obey your parents because you belong to the Lord, for this is the right thing to do. "Honor your father and mother." This is the first of the Ten Commandments that ends with a promise. And this is the promise: If you honor your father and mother, "you will live a long life, full of blessing." (Ephesians 6:1-3)*

RELATED QUESTIONS: *Can I be involved in both baseball and soccer? What's a good sport to be involved in?*

NOTE TO PARENTS: *It's not easy to know when to push kids into something and when to let them make the choice. Try thinking of several options that will meet your learning objectives for your children and then let them choose. Don't give in the first time that your kids complain about an activity, but also avoid pushing them into something that they dislike intensely. Remember, you want to find ways to meet your children's needs, not yours.*

Q: I LIKE PLAYING THE PIANO, BUT I HATE PRACTICING. SHOULD I QUIT?

104

A: Getting good at anything takes practice. Practicing usually isn't fun, but it is necessary. Keep practicing—don't quit. When you get good enough to play music that you enjoy, you'll really have fun playing the piano. This works the same way in other areas of life. You've probably heard that practice makes perfect. This means that the more you practice, the better you will get.

KEY VERSE: *So don't get tired of doing what is good. Don't get discouraged and give up, for we will reap a harvest of blessing at the appropriate time. (Galatians 6:9)*

RELATED VERSES: *Psalm 119:34; 1 Corinthians 9:25*

NOTE TO PARENTS: *If your children like the piano but don't want to practice, this will give you the opportunity to teach personal discipline. If your kids hate the instrument, recitals, and practicing, however, you may need to find another way to expose them to music. They might prefer playing another instrument, or they may enjoy simply listening to CDs and attending concerts.*

Q:

WHY DO MY PARENTS WANT ME TO BE INVOLVED IN SO MANY THINGS?

105

A: Your parents love you and want the best for you. They want you to have many experiences that will help you grow and be a more informed person. Because they don't know what you are going to be good at or what you're going to be interested in when you are older, they want you to try a lot of different activities now. You can learn a lot through music lessons, church choir, sports, and other activities outside of school. Everything you learn will help you enjoy life more. Be thankful that your parents are trying to help you learn as much as you can.

KEY VERSES: *You children must always obey your parents, for this is what pleases the Lord. Fathers, don't aggravate your children. If you do, they will become discouraged and quit trying. (Colossians 3:20-21)*

RELATED VERSE: *Proverbs 23:22*

NOTE TO PARENTS: *Children who ask this question may be feeling overwhelmed with their schedule. Being involved in too many activities can be dangerous for children because of the stress it creates. Children need time to relax and play even more than adults do. You may want to evaluate the number of activities and the kinds of activities you are expecting them to take part in.*

WHY DOES MY COACH CARE SO MUCH ABOUT WINNING? IT'S NOT FUN ANYMORE.

106

A: Sometimes winning becomes too important to people. In our society being number one seems to be most important. Coaches and parents can get caught up in this pressure. It's good to win, but it's also important to have fun playing a sport. If winning seems to be more important to your team than having fun, talk to your parents. Then they can talk with the coach. If nothing changes, you may want to ask your parents what they think about helping you get on a different team.

KEY VERSE: *So I saw that there is nothing better for people than to be happy in their work. That is why they are here! No one will bring them back from death to enjoy life in the future. (Ecclesiastes 3:22)*

NOTE TO PARENTS: *The pressure of having to win at a young age usually is not good. If your children are competitive, this may not be a problem. But most children are more interested in playing than in winning. Exposure to a high-pressure coach may burn out your child's interest in that sport. Changing to a different team may be the best solution.*

Q: HOW CAN I GET BETTER AT ART?

107

A: If you have talent in art, you will get better at it in the same way you get better at anything else—by practice. To get better at art, you need to do a variety of art projects. Ask your parents if you can get some art supplies for your birthday or Christmas. Then find creative ways to use things your parents are throwing out, such as old magazines and cardboard boxes. Get some scrap paper and spend time drawing or designing. You might ask your Sunday school teacher to help you find an adult at church who is artistic and would be willing to give you lessons. You may also ask your parents if there are art classes in your community that you can take.

KEY VERSE: *To those who use well what they are given, even more will be given, and they will have an abundance. But from those who are unfaithful, even what little they have will be taken away. (Matthew 25:29)*

RELATED VERSE: *Ephesians 6:7*

NOTE TO PARENTS: *When a child shows strong interest in art or music, Mom and Dad should look for ways to build on that interest and develop that talent. Outside of school, park districts and other community groups often provide classes and seminars where children—even the very young ones—can participate and further develop their skills.*

Q: I WANT TO BE WITH MY FRIENDS. WHY DO WE HAVE TO GO TO CHURCH SO MUCH?

108

A: Christians go to church to worship God, study the Bible, and be with other people who believe in Jesus. Church is a special place where you can learn more about God's love and how to please him. Churches also sponsor clubs and other children's activities. Remember, you can bring your friends to church. You can also make friends at church.

KEY VERSE: *I was glad when they said to me, "Let us go to the house of the Lord." (Psalm 122:1)*

RELATED VERSE: *Psalm 55:14*

NOTE TO PARENTS: *Be sensible about thinking and then insisting that you and your family are to be at the church every time the doors are open. You may have to miss some activities and programs for the sake of your family. On the other hand, don't give the impression that regular church attendance is optional. Make worship and Christian education a regular part of your family life. Also do whatever you can to make church attendance pleasant, such as allowing plenty of time to get ready beforehand.*

IN THE NEWS

Q: WHY DID GOD PUT LIGHTNING AND THUNDER AND ALL THAT DANGEROUS STUFF IN THE WORLD?

109

A: God created the world with natural forces that work for our good, and lightning is one of those natural forces. For example, the powerful electrical charge released in lightning makes nitrogen, which we need in the air we breathe. Thunder is simply the sound that lightning makes. Lightning is a good thing, not a bad thing.

But it is also dangerous. Lightning can hurt or kill someone who gets in the way of it. That is why we should not stand outside in a storm when lightning is doing its work.

Almost anything can be dangerous if used in the wrong way or if abused. Even a small rubber band can be dangerous if left on the floor where a baby is crawling. We need to respect nature and natural forces. This means avoiding very dangerous areas and acting wisely.

KEY VERSE: *He gives his sunlight to both the evil and the good, and he sends rain on the just and on the unjust, too. (Matthew 5:45)*

RELATED QUESTIONS: *Why does lightning hit people? Do thunder and lightning mean that God is angry?*

NOTE TO PARENTS: *People sometimes flaunt natural laws and act irresponsibly (like building homes on a floodplain, on a fault line, or near a volcano). The Bible says that "fear of the Lord is the beginning of knowledge" (Proverbs 1:7). When we live our lives in cooperation with God's principles and laws of creation, we are using wisdom.*

Q: WHY DOES GOD KILL NATURE WITH FOREST FIRES?

110

A: Forest fires don't kill nature. They are part of the life cycle that God built into our world. Raging forest fires can destroy many thousands of trees and wildlife. But forest fires also help life continue. For example, they burn away dead growth and open seed pods, such as those of jack pines, which can't be opened any other way. Forest fires are a little like lightning— they may be dangerous, but they do important work.

Some forest fires start naturally, and some are started by people. We should not try to start forest fires just to destroy property. And we should try to keep them from damaging property or endangering people's lives. But some fires start naturally, and we know now that they are necessary. This is just part of God's plan for us and our world.

KEY VERSES: *Then God said, "Let the land burst forth with every sort of grass and seed-bearing plant. And let there be trees that grow seed-bearing fruit. The seeds will then produce the kinds of plants and trees from which they came." And so it was. The land was filled with seed-bearing plants and trees, and their seeds produced plants and trees of like kind. And God saw that it was good. (Genesis 1:11-12)*

RELATED VERSES: *Psalm 83:14; Psalm 96:12; James 3:5*

RELATED QUESTIONS: *Why do forest fires happen? How do forest fires start? How do forest fires stop?*

NOTE TO PARENTS: *Whenever your children ask about fire, be careful not to overplay fear to keep them from it. Fire can be used for good purposes, even though it is dangerous. Simply teach them to respect these dangers, to use fire responsibly, and to handle it wisely.*

Q: WHY DO FLOODS AND HURRICANES KILL INNOCENT PEOPLE?

EMERGENCY FLOOD RELIEF

EEOOEEOO
EEOOEEOO

111

A: Most floods, and all hurricanes, are natural disasters that can't be prevented. They are simply events that happen when water strikes with great force (for example, from storms at sea, heavy rains, or melting snow). The forces of nature go to work, and those forces are very powerful.

Sometimes people die in these natural disasters because they have not listened to a warning. Some live too near the water and in areas that flood easily. Some ignore storm warnings and stay in the path of danger when they should leave. Some even try to get *close* to a powerful storm, risking their lives because they think it will be exciting. Too many people die in floods and hurricanes because they are foolish.

But others die through no fault of their own; they are in the wrong place at the wrong time. It is not because God overlooked them; it is because we live in a broken world. We have suffering and death because of sin.

Deaths from floods and hurricanes are tragedies. That is why we need to be wise and do what we can to avoid unnecessary risks. As long as we have sin in this world we will have these dangers, and we need to avoid them.

KEY VERSE: *Anyone who listens to my teaching and obeys me is wise, like a person who builds a house on solid rock. (Matthew 7:24)*

RELATED VERSES: *Matthew 7:25-27*

RELATED QUESTIONS: *Why do big floods happen? Why do tornadoes happen? Why do hurricanes happen? How fast do tornadoes turn? Why don't people go before their house gets flooded? Why do floods and tornadoes kill people?*

Q: WHY DOES GOD SEND EARTHQUAKES?

112

A: Like hurricanes, earthquakes are a natural part of the way the earth works. Huge pieces of the earth's surface, called tectonic plates, are shifting and rubbing against each other all the time. Sometimes their movements release great amounts of energy stored up in the friction between them. The release of this energy produces an earthquake. It is not that God sends earthquakes so much as that they happen as part of the world God has made.

Earthquakes can do a lot of damage to buildings and other structures not made to handle the mighty rumblings and shocks. If possible, people who live in earthquake areas should have homes built with earthquakes in mind. They should also plan how they will get to safety the next time an earthquake happens. This is simply an example of planning wisely and being careful.

KEY VERSE: *When the earth quakes and its people live in turmoil, I am the one who keeps its foundations firm. (Psalm 75:3)*

RELATED QUESTIONS: *How do earthquakes happen? Why do earthquakes have to happen? Why do only certain areas get earthquakes?*

NOTE TO PARENTS: *If you live in an area prone to earthquakes, teach your children what to do in the event of a tremor. Be familiar with basic safety steps—including where to go and what not to do—and explain them to your children. You can even make a game of practicing them!*

Q: WHY DO PEOPLE DIE IN HOT WEATHER?

EMERGENCY LEMONADE RELIEF

EEOO EEOO
EEOO EEOO

113

A: Temperatures over 100 degrees Fahrenheit (35 degrees Celsius) put a lot of stress on the human body. In hot weather, bodies need more water than normal because they lose water more quickly. Older people and those who are sick suffer the most, because their bodies are not as strong as younger, healthier people. Most of the people who die in hot weather become overheated because they can't get cooled off. If they would go to a cooler place or to a building with air-conditioning, they could cool off.

This is one way people can look out for each other. If you have older relatives, make sure they have a way to get cool on a really hot day.

KEY VERSE: *O God, you are my God; I earnestly search for you. My soul thirsts for you; my whole body longs for you in this parched and weary land where there is no water. (Psalm 63:1)*

RELATED VERSES: *Deuteronomy 8:15; Job 6:17-18; Isaiah 32:1-2*

RELATED QUESTIONS: *What is the hottest place in the world? What is the coldest place in the world?*

NOTE TO PARENTS: *Children tend to think of themselves as invulnerable and often don't know the dangers that high heat can pose. Make sure your kids know how to handle themselves in hot weather. They should drink plenty of fluids, try to stay cool, stay out of the sun, and limit their exercise.*

Q: WHO FEEDS PEOPLE WHO DON'T HAVE ENOUGH TO EAT?

114

A: Although there is plenty of food in the world, thousands of people go hungry every day. Maybe they live far from food or they just don't have money to buy food.

Many people who care about this work hard to feed those who don't have enough to eat. This is the main purpose of many relief organizations. Some government agencies, churches, and other organizations also help. If you know of a hungry family, you could take them a bag of groceries or a special meal. You could also support the work of a Christian organization that is working with the poor. Some people sponsor children through agencies; some donate money; others take food to food pantries; and some donate time at homeless shelters, soup kitchens, and other places that help poor people.

KEY VERSES: *Suppose you see a brother or sister who needs food or clothing, and you say, "Well, good-bye and God bless you; stay warm and eat well"—but then you don't give that person any food or clothing. What good does that do? (James 2:15-16)*

RELATED VERSES: *Proverbs 28:27; Romans 12:8-9*

RELATED QUESTIONS: *Why don't we help people who don't have enough to eat? Why don't some people in the world have enough to eat? Why aren't people generous to give food to people who don't have enough to eat? Why can't we give our food to hungry people?*

NOTE TO PARENTS: *It is good to get involved as a family to help meet the needs of the poor. It helps people in a tangible way and also shows God's love to them. Consider options available to you through your church or another organization that you trust.*

Q: WHY DO PEOPLE COMMIT CRIMES?

115

A: The main reason people commit crimes is that they are selfish. They want what others have and take it by force. Another big reason is anger. People get so angry that they lose their temper and do things that they would not normally do. Both selfishness and uncontrolled anger are sin.

Crime happens when people get cut off from God and his love. Some people do not know God at all and do not know that they can trust him to take care of them. Some people know him but lose touch with him, then fail to trust and obey him. God's way is for us to know him, to ask and trust him for the things we need, and then to love and help others. If everyone did things God's way all the time, crime would never happen. That is why we need to trust God to provide for us instead of selfishly trying to get what we want regardless of how it affects others.

KEY VERSE: *When they refused to acknowledge God, he abandoned them to their evil minds and let them do things that should never be done. (Romans 1:28)*

RELATED VERSES: *Proverbs 4:16-17; Romans 1:29-32; 3:23; Ephesians 4:26-27, 31-32*

NOTE TO PARENTS: *It is important to teach children to talk their way through conflicts with others instead of forcing their way by hitting, screaming, or threatening. On the playground, at school, and among siblings, they will get into conflicts of will every day. Most things are not worth fighting for. It is OK to try to persuade; it is not OK to use force on those who disagree. Remind them that they can control their temper (Proverbs 12:16).*

Q: WHAT ARE CRIME WAVES?

116

A: You know what a wave is—it's a whole bunch of water moving in the same direction all at once. A crime wave is a whole bunch of crime all happening at once.

Crime waves often start when many people think they can get away with their crimes. For example, an upsetting event happens, and a mob of people react in some criminal way, like breaking store windows and stealing the merchandise. Or there is a natural disaster that leaves stores open and unprotected, and local people loot them, thinking that they won't get caught. Or a new crime comes along, like doing drugs, and many people do it.

Don't be fooled by the popularity of a crime wave. Wrong is wrong, no matter how many people do it. A crime is a crime, even if the police never catch anyone doing it. It is not possible to get away with a crime, because "you can't ignore God and get away with it. You will always reap what you sow!" (Galatians 6:7).

KEY VERSE: *My child, if sinners entice you, turn your back on them! (Proverbs 1:10)*

RELATED VERSES: *Proverbs 1:11-19; 4:14; Matthew 27:16*

RELATED QUESTIONS: *Why are there crime waves? How does crime happen? Why is crime worse in some places?*

Q: WHY IS THE WORLD SO VIOLENT AND EVIL?

117

A: Sin is the root cause of all evil. Because people sin, the world is filled with sin and evil. It has been this way since Adam and Eve's first sin. In fact, God flooded the world in Noah's day because of violence and evil. These things are not new.

In some ways it may seem that violence is worse today than in the past. Weapons are more destructive than ever before. There are more guns and knives and more ways of hurting people than ever before. As these weapons get more powerful, so does the power to hurt others.

But in reality, violence and evil come out of evil hearts that are separated from God, and the world has always had that. As long as people rebel against God, we will have violence and evil in the world.

KEY VERSE: *Don't let evil get the best of you, but conquer evil by doing good. (Romans 12:21)*

RELATED VERSES: *Genesis 6:11-13; 1 John 5:19*

RELATED QUESTIONS: *What percent of the world is violent? Why do people do bad things? Is Satan the only cause for evil? Why are there bad things in the world? How come people are doing so many bad things in the world? Why do they show so many guns on the news?*

NOTE TO PARENTS: *When your children ask a question like this, make sure they get a balanced view. Talk about all the good that is happening in the world. Many believers are telling others about Christ, helping to relieve suffering through health care, serving as missionaries, praying for leaders, and working behind the scenes to achieve good. God has not abandoned our world.*

Q: WHY ARE THERE SO MANY ACCIDENTS AND PEOPLE GETTING KILLED?

DO NOT DISTURB. DEEP IN THOUGHT

118

A: Because of sin in the world. When God created the world, everything was perfect. But when the first people disobeyed God, sin threw things out of order. This is what it means to say we live in a *fallen world*. It is full of dangers. If it weren't for sin, we would not have suffering or death at all.

Some of our own creations have also brought new dangers. The fact that we can go faster in cars and planes means that accidents can have bigger and worse results. People also have lots of accidents when they are in a hurry. As they rush from place to place, they run into others.

It is important to be careful. This means looking both ways before crossing streets, watching where you are going, wearing seat belts, and using common sense. As long as accidents happen in this world, we must be careful.

KEY VERSE: *A prudent person foresees the danger ahead and takes precautions. The simpleton goes blindly on and suffers the consequences. (Proverbs 27:12)*

RELATED VERSES: *Proverbs 1:32-33; Luke 13:4-5*

RELATED QUESTIONS: *How come the news is so boring? Why don't they just put in the newspaper what they were going to put on TV?*

NOTE TO PARENTS: *Whenever you pray with your children about God protecting them, ask God for the wisdom and common sense they need to live safely. This helps them remember that they have a role to play in staying safe.*

CULTURES
AND
COUNTRIES

119

A: Some names sound strange to you, but they sound fine in the countries that have them. Names have meaning inside their own cultures. For example, we might think that a name like Botswana or Bosnia-Herzegovina sounds weird because we don't live there and don't know what the name means. But in those countries, New York, Vancouver, Saskatchewan, and Alaska probably sound silly too.

KEY VERSE: *That area, too, was once considered the land of the Rephaites, though the Ammonites referred to them as Zamzummites. (Deuteronomy 2:20)*

RELATED VERSES: *Judges 12:5-6; Colossians 3:11; Revelation 5:9-13*

Q: WHY DO PEOPLE IN DIFFERENT COUNTRIES HAVE DIFFERENT CUSTOMS THAN WE DO?

120

A: One reason is that many years ago there was very little communication among countries that were far apart. People living in Africa, for example, didn't know anything about people living in Asia, and people in Australia didn't know about people in America. The people in each country developed their own way of doing things without knowing how others around the world were doing them.

Another reason for many of the differences is climate. In places where the weather is always hot, people will dress and eat in ways that make sense in hot areas. Eskimos dress in furs and eat lots of fish because that's what they need to wear and that's what kind of food is available in their climate.

Always show respect for people who are not like you. It is a simple way to honor and learn to enjoy the marvelous variety of people and nations God has made.

KEY VERSE: *I try to find common ground with everyone so that I might bring them to Christ. (1 Corinthians 9:22)*

RELATED VERSE: *1 Peter 2:17*

RELATED QUESTION: *Why are people in other countries different?*

NOTE TO PARENTS: *Be sure to distinguish between moral issues and cultural ones. It is wrong to steal or hate, no matter what your culture is. But differences in dress, food, language, music, special celebrations, and even the way a family operates are not wrong. Speak positively of these differences.*

Q: DO PEOPLE KEEP THEIR CULTURE WHEN THEY MOVE TO A DIFFERENT COUNTRY?

121

A: At first they do. In fact, people who move from one country to another often try hard to keep the customs and traditions of their home country. But it is difficult to do, because few of the people around them live the same way, and it takes a big group of people all living the same way to support a culture.

For example, if the people want to speak their native language, they have to talk with others who also speak their language. If they want to eat the food of their homeland, they need to know where they can buy the ingredients. If they celebrate the holidays they grew up with, they may be the only ones doing so.

In most families that move to another country or culture, this is a real struggle. People like that need all the hospitality and welcoming they can get from friends and neighbors.

KEY VERSE: *Don't forget to show hospitality to strangers, for some who have done this have entertained angels without realizing it! (Hebrews 13:2)*

RELATED VERSES: *Genesis 12:1; Romans 12:13; 1 Peter 4:9*

RELATED QUESTIONS: *Why do people immigrate? How could Adam and Eve's children cross the sea to North America?*

NOTE TO PARENTS: *Some children who move from one country to another will treasure the habits and customs of the country they left. Other children will more readily adapt to the customs and habits of their new homeland. Usually this is a matter of personality and disposition. A parent should guide each child through the trauma of moving in the ways that are appropriate for that child. Be sensitive to the different types of personalities and how each person reacts to moving.*

CULTURES AND COUNTRIES

Q: WHY DO PEOPLE HAVE TO SPEAK DIFFERENT LANGUAGES?

122

A:

It all started at a place called Babel in Babylonia, where Iraq is today. During the time of Adam and Eve and Noah, everyone in the world spoke the same language. But shortly after Noah and his family emerged from the ark, the people of the world gathered together to build a tower as a monument to their own greatness. They had completely forgotten about God. So God caused their language to divide into dialects. God changed the languages to confuse the people so they wouldn't finish building the Tower of Babel. People who spoke the same language stayed together, moved away, and settled in different areas all over the world. Ever since then, languages have been part of what makes countries different from each other. And even within countries, different ethnic groups often speak different languages.

KEY VERSES: *In that way, the Lord scattered them all over the earth; and that ended the building of the city. That is why the city was called Babel, because it was there that the Lord confused the people by giving them many languages, thus scattering them across the earth. (Genesis 11:8-9)*

RELATED QUESTIONS: *Why do people in different countries speak different? Why are there so many different kinds of languages? Why can't there just be one language?*

Q: WHY DO SOME FAMILIES SPEAK MORE THAN ONE LANGUAGE?

123

A: Some families live in parts of the world where all people speak more than one language. Many Europeans, especially those in small countries, are in this situation. People in Germany, for example, live quite close to people in France and England, and they will probably need to speak to English speakers and French speakers many times throughout their lives. So as they grow up, they learn to speak English and French as well as German. That's three languages right there.

Some people live in countries that have two or more official languages. Canada has two—English and French. Switzerland has three—French, German, and Italian. In countries like these, people usually speak the language most common to their area.

Some people live in cultures where they did not grow up. They have had to learn a new language so they can talk to the people in that land. This is what happens when people come to North America from Mexico, for example, or when people move from North America to Switzerland.

Many missionaries need to learn another language so they can tell people about God in their own language.

KEY VERSE: *Then Eliakim son of Hilkiah, Shebna, and Joah said to the king's representative, "Please speak to us in Aramaic, for we understand it well. Don't speak in Hebrew, for the people on the wall will hear." (2 Kings 18:26)*

RELATED VERSES: *Daniel 7:14; Acts 2:6*

RELATED QUESTIONS: *Why do some people have to speak two languages? What was the first language ever spoken on the earth? What language did Goliath speak? What language did Jesus speak?*

Q: WHY DO PEOPLE IN OTHER COUNTRIES EAT DIFFERENT FOOD?

124

A: People choose what foods to eat for many reasons. Sometimes they eat the foods that they can get easily and that don't cost very much money. A rice farmer, for example, probably would eat a lot of rice. Some foods are very expensive because they have to be grown a long way away or because a certain food is very scarce.

Some foods are chosen because of culture and habit. In some countries, the people have learned to enjoy eating very spicy foods. In other countries, everyone likes fish. And in still other countries, people eat a lot of meat and potatoes. What people eat is a matter of tradition, habit, and personal taste.

KEY VERSES: *Every one of these depends on you to give them their food as they need it. When you supply it, they gather it. You open your hand to feed them, and they are satisfied. (Psalm 104:27-28)*

RELATED VERSE: *Isaiah 25:6*

RELATED QUESTIONS: *Why do some people like sweet and sour or spicy foods? Why do people in different countries eat different foods for feasts?*

NOTE TO PARENTS: *A fun way to help your children learn about and be more accepting of other cultures is to introduce them to different ethnic foods. Take them to an ethnic restaurant, make a meal from an ethnic cookbook, or invite a friend to show you how to make a favorite ethnic dish.*

Q: IN OTHER COUNTRIES, WHY DO PEOPLE BURP ALOUD AFTER MEALS?

125

A: In some countries, burping aloud after a meal shows that you enjoyed the meal. In other countries, it is more polite to say something nice about the meal instead of burping. Different groups of people have different ways of life. It's a good idea to show respect for the people when you travel to another country. Find out which of your behaviors may offend others. That way you can try hard to avoid embarrassing yourself and your hosts.

KEY VERSES: *In those days it was the custom in Israel for anyone transferring a right of purchase to remove his sandal and hand it to the other party. This publicly validated the transaction. So the other family redeemer drew off his sandal as he said to Boaz, "You buy the land." (Ruth 4:7-8)*

RELATED VERSE: *1 Peter 2:17*

RELATED QUESTIONS: *How come in other countries it's all right to burp aloud? Why, when little babies burp, parents say, "Good girl/boy!" but when they get bigger and burp, parents get mad? How come some people in different countries eat with their mouths open and without forks? Why don't people in some countries use tables?*

Q: WHY ARE SOME COUNTRIES RICH AND OTHERS POOR?

126

A: Some countries are very rich and others very poor for many reasons. Wealthy countries often have many natural resources (such as oil, gold, rich fisheries, or tourist attractions) that bring them great wealth. They also have economic systems that reward people for making and selling goods and services; they attract buyers with the things they make and sell. And they have laws that protect people from being cheated.

Other countries don't have these things, and that makes them poor. Perhaps they don't have the natural resources that people want to buy. Or perhaps they have the resources, but the economic system makes it hard for people to sell them or for buyers to buy them. Also, some countries have been hurt by war, hurricanes, earthquakes, famines, or other tragedies.

It takes time and cooperation for a country to change from being poor to being rich. Everyone has to work together and support free trade. Everyone has to make rules and keep them. That is one of the ways God rewards people who abide by his laws—obeying the laws keeps things orderly. This is just another example of God's love at work. When we follow God's principles, life works better.

KEY VERSE: *Hard workers have plenty of food; playing around brings poverty. (Proverbs 28:19)*

RELATED VERSES: *Job 12:23; Proverbs 28:15-16; Luke 1:52-53*

RELATED QUESTIONS: *Why are some countries so big and others so small? Why do people in some countries go barefoot and in others they wear shoes? Why can't people wear shorts instead of business suits? Why do some people wear sandals and other people wear shoes?*

Q: WHY IS THERE A McDONALD'S IN ALMOST EVERY COUNTRY?

127

A: Some companies, like McDonald's and Coca-Cola, can be found in many places around the world because they have worked hard to sell their products in those places. They have hired people to set up factories, stores, or distributors in other countries. They have signed contracts with other companies to help them. These companies keep doing this until it seems they have products in almost every country.

Another reason is communication among people around the world. Television, e-mail, the Internet, long-distance telephone connections, and air travel allow people to know a lot about those who live a long way away from them. They learn about other people's customs, products, food, and stores. Some decide to open a branch store in a faraway town. Modern technology has made it easier than ever to do business all over the world.

KEY VERSE: *Judah and Israel traded for your wares, offering wheat from Minnith, early figs, honey, oil, and balm. (Ezekiel 27:17)*

RELATED VERSES: *Ezekiel 27:1-36; Luke 12:16-19*

RELATED QUESTION: *Why are some things the same in almost every country?*

Q: I DON'T GET IT—WHY ARE PEOPLE PREJUDICED?

128

A: The biggest reason for prejudice is fear of people who are different. People tend to fear what they don't know or understand, including other people or their customs. People also tend to think badly of people and customs that they don't understand. People become prejudiced when they believe false ideas about what others are like.

We do not need to fear variety in the way people cook, dress, and talk. We need to appreciate these differences and not judge or criticize people just because they do not do these things our way.

Some people also believe—wrongly—that certain kinds of people are better or more important than others. This is called *racism*. People who have this perspective don't realize that God created *all* people in his image. Every person who has ever been born is equally important and valuable. No one is better or deserving of superior treatment.

Jesus wants us to love and respect others, even if we don't know or understand them. We should not think badly of people just because we don't understand them. We should not be prejudiced.

KEY VERSE: *God does not show favoritism. (Romans 2:11)*

RELATED VERSES: *Acts 10:34; Galatians 3:28*

RELATED QUESTIONS: *Why don't some people like people who are different from them? If Adam and Eve are the father and mother of everyone on earth, then why isn't everyone your brother or sister?*

NOTE TO PARENTS: *Children learn prejudice by watching others show it; few parents or others actively teach it. We need to be careful to not use prejudiced language, tell prejudiced jokes, or avoid people for prejudiced reasons.*

RELIGION

Q: WHY DOES THE WORLD HAVE DIFFERENT RELIGIONS?

129

A: Various religions exist for many different reasons. Most cultures know about God, but many that don't know him have tried to explain him in their own ways; they have formed their own religions.

Many people do not want to believe that there is only one way to God, so they start their own way and try to get others to join them. All of those people need to hear about God's love for them and about Jesus' dying for them.

Christianity also has many different *denominations*. A denomination is a group of churches. Some of these groups formed because the people were all from a certain country and culture or spoke a certain language (for example, German Baptists or Swedish Covenant). Other denominations exist because they hold their church services differently from others or believe in expressing their faith in a specific way.

The Bible tells us, however, that Jesus Christ is the *only* way to God. Christians may go to many different churches that speak different languages or have certain types of services as long as their beliefs and worship center on Christ and God's Word. All Christians should love and appreciate each other and work together despite their differences.

KEY VERSE: *Do not worship any other gods besides me. (Exodus 20:3)*

RELATED VERSES: *Exodus 20:4-6; John 14:6; Acts 17:16-34*

NOTE TO PARENTS: *When children focus on what is "wrong" with how other Christians believe or worship, redirect their attention to their own lives. Their energy should be spent on becoming like Christ, not on correcting others.*

Q: WHAT KIND OF HOLY BOOKS DO PEOPLE OF OTHER RELIGIONS HAVE?

A: Many religions have books of instructions or books that help people understand their own religion. Most of these religions have many, many books, not just one. These books explain the beliefs and practices of these religions.

In some ways, this is similar to how Christians use the Bible, but the Bible is also unique. The Bible has many prophecies, or predictions of the future, that have come true exactly as predicted. It also tells of many, many places and events that archaeologists have discovered to be true and accurate. Other "holy books" don't survive all these kinds of tests. The more we learn about the past, the more we learn that we can trust what the Bible says.

KEY VERSE: *Philip went off to look for Nathanael and told him, "We have found the very person Moses and the prophets wrote about! His name is Jesus, the son of Joseph from Nazareth." (John 1:45)*

RELATED VERSES: *Deuteronomy 18:20; Joshua 1:7-8; Revelation 22:8-9*

RELATED QUESTIONS: *Why do people of other religions make holy books? Why do people of other religions think their books are holy books?*

Q: DOES GOD LOVE PEOPLE WHO DON'T PRAY?

131

A: God loves all people, even those who do not love him. The Bible tells of some unbelieving kings who prayed and to whom God listened. God is delighted whenever someone honors him, calls out to him, or expresses a need for him. And he invites people to come to him because he loves them; his love does not depend on whether or not a person prays.

But that does not mean that God loves everything that people do. Just because God loves people does not make all people right or good in his sight. Having a relationship with Jesus gives a person a relationship with God that not just anyone can have.

That is why God wants us to pray. It allows us to enjoy our relationship with God, to benefit from his friendship, and to see him work in our life.

KEY VERSE: *Then they cried out to the Lord, Jonah's God. "O Lord," they pleaded, "don't make us die for this man's sin. And don't hold us responsible for his death, because it isn't our fault. O Lord, you have sent this storm upon him for your own good reasons." (Jonah 1:14)*

RELATED VERSES: *Psalm 17:1; Jeremiah 29:13; Acts 17:23, 27-31*

RELATED QUESTION: *If Hindus believe in many gods and Buddhists don't believe in any god, how can they live in the same country?*

Q: WHY DO PEOPLE WORSHIP IDOLS INSTEAD OF GOD?

132

A: Idols are simply pictures or statues of imaginary gods. Actually, most people who have idols don't worship the idols but the gods they represent. Some people, however, think that an idol itself can help them.

People want to believe in things that they can see and touch, so they make things they can see. But we cannot see God because God is spirit. As Christians, we do not make or worship idols because idols take our attention away from worshiping the one true God.

KEY VERSE: *No one has ever seen God. But his only Son, who is himself God, is near to the Father's heart; he has told us about him. (John 1:18)*

RELATED VERSES: *Exodus 20:3-4; Psalm 135:15-18; Isaiah 44:9-11*

RELATED QUESTIONS: *What's an idol? What are idols made of? Why do some people pray to objects? Why do people in other countries worship different idols?*

Q: WHY IS BEING GOOD NOT ENOUGH TO GET SOMEONE INTO HEAVEN?

133

A: It is impossible to be good enough to get into heaven. Every person sins, and even one sin is too many for heaven. Heaven is perfect because God is perfect—there is no sin at all in God's presence. A person would have to be perfect to get into heaven.

That is why we need Jesus. Only Jesus can accept us into God's presence by forgiving our sin.

We are each like a pane of glass in a window. If even one tiny corner of it is broken, it is broken. We need a miracle to make us whole again. We need to believe in Jesus and invite him to save us. Then we can have our sins forgiven and be ready for heaven.

KEY VERSE: *As the Scriptures say, "No one is good—not even one." (Romans 3:10)*

RELATED VERSES: *Psalm 14:1-3; Isaiah 1:18; Romans 3:9-18*

RELATED QUESTIONS: *If you did everything right and you were really nice to people, would you go to heaven? Why do people think that even if you're a good person that's not enough to get you to heaven?*

WARS
AND
RUMORS
OF WAR

Q: WHY DO COUNTRIES FIGHT WARS WITH EACH OTHER?

134

A: A war is fought when countries disagree and can't work out their problems by talking together. Sometimes a war will begin when both countries want the same thing, like a certain piece of land. Instead of talking it out, they fight. Other times, a war will begin when one country wants to take over another country.

God wants us to love others and try to get along with others. Many wars could be avoided if everyone followed God's instructions for loving others. And if each of us chooses to love God and others, we can prevent fights and make the world a little more peaceful.

KEY VERSES: *What is causing the quarrels and fights among you? Isn't it the whole army of evil desires at war within you? You want what you don't have, so you scheme and kill to get it. You are jealous for what others have, and you can't possess it, so you fight and quarrel to take it away from them. And yet the reason you don't have what you want is that you don't ask God for it. (James 4:1-2)*

RELATED VERSES: *Psalm 27:3; Proverbs 30:33; Matthew 24:6; James 4:2-3*

RELATED QUESTIONS: *What is the point of having war if all you're doing is risking getting yourself killed? Why can't people stop fighting wars? How come so many people in the world go to war? Why does God let people shoot each other?*

135

A: Dictators push people around because they like to have power and control over others. One of the most common sins that people commit is to use power to force people to do things their way. Because dictators are in control of everything in the country, they have a lot of power. Pushing people around is their way of abusing that power. Dictators who abuse their power are evil, and God will punish them in the end.

The Bible teaches us that the proper way to lead others is to serve them and put their interests ahead of your own. Whenever you get a chance to be in charge, even of younger brothers or sisters, think of what is best for them and do the fun things they want to do.

KEY VERSE: *When the wicked are in authority, sin increases. But the godly will live to see the tyrant's downfall. (Proverbs 29:16)*

RELATED VERSES: *Proverbs 28:2, 15; 29:2, 4; Isaiah 10:1*

RELATED QUESTIONS: *What are dictatorships? What do dictators do? Why do dictators tell you what to do? Why didn't God kill Hitler? If Hitler knew he was going to be mean, why did he want to govern Germany? Why isn't there a world leader?*

NOTE TO PARENTS: *Parental authority is the first leadership example that children have. Teach them to lead others by demonstrating service-motivated leadership.*

Q: WHY DO COUNTRIES HAVE ARMIES, NAVIES, AND AIR FORCES?

136

A: It is true that some countries have armies, navies, and air forces mainly so they can attack others. But most countries have armed forces only as a defense against invasion. Their forces protect the country from other countries that might want to go to war against them.

In some countries armed forces can also help in peacetime. The soldiers are used to keep order inside the country during protests and riots, and to rescue and help people during natural disasters like floods and hurricanes.

It is important to honor those who risk their lives to protect us. Most countries do this by setting aside a Memorial Day, Remembrance Day, or another holiday for people to remember the people in their armed forces. Remember to show your appreciation the next time this holiday comes around. They are "authorities sent by God to help you."

KEY VERSE: *The authorities are sent by God to help you. But if you are doing something wrong, of course you should be afraid, for you will be punished. The authorities are established by God for that very purpose, to punish those who do wrong. (Romans 13:4)*

RELATED VERSES: *Deuteronomy 20:1; Psalm 20:7; Amos 1:3-15; Romans 13:1-7*

RELATED QUESTIONS: *Why doesn't someone take away all the guns and tell people to love and live in peace instead? Why doesn't the government say, "No abortions, no killing, and no wars—share!"? Why do people even make weapons?*

Q: WHY ARE NUCLEAR WEAPONS EVEN AROUND?

137

A: Nuclear weapons were invented during World War II to gain an advantage over the Axis powers (Germany, Japan, and Italy). The government of the United States hired scientists to build a bomb that would be so powerful that the Japanese would have to surrender.

Because these weapons can kill hundreds of thousands of people at once, people all over the world have been working to get rid of them. They feel that we will only destroy ourselves if we use them.

Others know that these weapons make them powerful, so they work to keep the ones they have, or they make new ones. They feel that they would be defenseless without nuclear weapons.

This is just one reason God commands us to be kind, to forgive, and to return cruelty with kindness. Whenever we allow conflicts to escalate, or get worse, we build bigger weapons and do even more terrible things. God's way is better.

KEY VERSES: *When they refused to acknowledge God, he abandoned them to their evil minds and let them do things that should never be done. Their lives became full of every kind of wickedness, sin, greed, hate, envy, murder, fighting, deception, malicious behavior, and gossip. (Romans 1:28-29)*

RELATED VERSES: *Proverbs 3:25-26; 15:1*

RELATED QUESTIONS: *Why do people want to make weapons to destroy the world? Why do countries have nuclear weapons?*

NOTE TO PARENTS: *The basic principles that help avoid war are the same ones that help brothers and sisters get along. Peace starts at home.*

Q: WHY DO SOME COUNTRIES SPLIT APART?

138

A: Usually countries split apart when a group of people within the country wants to rule itself. It does not want to be part of the larger country anymore. Why would a group want to break away like that? Because different groups of people have different ways of life. People want to govern themselves, and certain groups don't want to be governed by other groups that have different ways of life. Sometimes groups get forced together under the same government against their will, such as in the former Soviet Union. Eventually the people's desire to govern themselves can cause the country to split.

KEY VERSES: *And I have provided a permanent homeland for my people Israel, a secure place where they will never be disturbed. It will be their own land where wicked nations won't oppress them as they did in the past, from the time I appointed judges to rule my people. And I will keep you safe from all your enemies. (2 Samuel 7:10-11)*

RELATED VERSES: *Mark 13:7; Luke 19:14*

RELATED QUESTIONS: *How come countries break away from their old country and become a new country? How come two countries become one country? When two countries join together, do they start their age all over again?*

NOTE TO PARENTS: *It is important to teach our children to respect the will and desires of others, and a brother-and-sister relationship is a good place for them to start. If a brother or sister says, "Stop teasing me," or "Please stop tickling me," or "Stop crowding me," then the other should know that he or she must stop. Make respect for others a basic rule in your house.*

Q: IS GOD HAPPY FOR ONE COUNTRY AND SAD FOR THE OTHER AT THE END OF A WAR?

139

A: God is saddened by all sin and death. In most wars, nobody wins. People from both sides are hurt and killed. Property is destroyed. Countries, cities, neighborhoods, and families are torn apart. God is not happy with any of it. He is sad about all the destruction caused by sin, including war.

But sometimes God does send war as a punishment for evil. In the Old Testament we read that some nations suffered in wars as a punishment for their sins against others. And sometimes war seems to be the only way to stop an evil dictator or an evil government. But that doesn't mean that God is happy to see nations go to war. He much prefers that people obey him, get along with each other, and avoid war altogether.

KEY VERSE: *The Lord will settle international disputes. All the nations will beat their swords into plowshares and their spears into pruning hooks. All wars will stop, and military training will come to an end. (Micah 4:3)*

RELATED VERSES: *Amos 5:6-7, 14-15*

RELATED QUESTIONS: *Who started World War I and II? If God loves the world, why do wars happen? How come wars are still going on in the world? Why don't people help people from other countries and give to them, instead of fighting them?*

LEADERS
AND
POLITICS

Q: WHAT ARE POLITICS?

VOTE

WE'RE HERE FOR THE RALLY.

POLITICAL RALLY

140

A: *Politics* is the word we use to describe governing or ruling. Politics is when people deal with one another in government. It includes trying to persuade someone else to vote your way. One part of politics involves electing government leaders. The political activities leading up to an election are called a "campaign." In a political campaign, the people who are trying to get elected try to persuade voters to vote for them through speeches, advertisements, debates, and so forth.

Governments are an important part of God's design for the world. God wants all rulers to obey him and for citizens to obey the government's laws. That is why voters should think carefully and pray often about whom to vote for. We want to pick the best rulers—the ones who will do the best job.

KEY VERSE: *Now look around among yourselves, brothers, and select seven men who are well respected and are full of the Holy Spirit and wisdom. We will put them in charge of this business. (Acts 6:3)*

RELATED VERSES: *1 Kings 3:10-14; Esther 4:14; 7:1-10; Proverbs 29:2; Matthew 27:15-26; Acts 12:1-3*

Q: WHY CAN'T CHILDREN VOTE?

141

A: Young children are not allowed to vote because they have not had enough experience and education to have earned the right to vote. Also, they are not involved enough in society. In other words, they don't pay taxes, own land, drive a car, or run a business. In a sense, a person earns the right to vote by growing up.

The best way to become a good voter is to love and obey God with all your heart. If you know what God wants for your country, you will make better voting decisions than if you didn't know what God wants. Until then, you can pray for your leaders and voters, asking God to give them wisdom.

KEY VERSE: *Don't let anyone think less of you because you are young. Be an example to all believers in what you teach, in the way you live, in your love, your faith, and your purity. (1 Timothy 4:12)*

RELATED VERSES: *Exodus 20:12; 1 Kings 12:8-9; Proverbs 3:5-8; 1 Timothy 2:2*

RELATED QUESTION: *When people vote for who they want to be their leader, what if they don't want any of them?*

Q: WHAT IS DEMOCRACY?

142

A:

Democracy is a type of government in which the citizens of a country elect the men and women who will lead them. These elected leaders are called representatives because they represent the people of that country—they speak for the citizens. In the election for each office (such as governor, mayor, senator, or council person), the person who gets the most votes wins the election and holds that office until the next election. In every election, the citizens can elect new leaders if they want to. Wise citizens choose their leaders very carefully, because a leader's character will determine whether he or she is a just ruler.

Be sure to pray for your country's leaders. They need God's wisdom all the time.

KEY VERSES: *When he sits on the throne as king, he must copy these laws on a scroll for himself in the presence of the Levitical priests. He must always keep this copy of the law with him and read it daily as long as he lives. That way he will learn to fear the Lord his God by obeying all the terms of this law. This regular reading will prevent him from becoming proud and acting as if he is above his fellow citizens. It will also prevent him from turning away from these commands in the smallest way. This will ensure that he and his descendants will reign for many generations in Israel. (Deuteronomy 17:18-20)*

RELATED VERSES: *Psalm 72:15; Proverbs 29:4; 1 Timothy 2:2*

NOTE TO PARENTS: *In our society, most heroes are musicians, actors, and sports figures. It is good to help our children expand their list of heroes to include leaders with exceptional character. Thinking about leaders this way helps prepare children for voting and being leaders.*

Q: WHAT IS COMMUNISM?

CALL-MOO-ISM

MOoo° MOooo?

143

A: Communism is a system in which people own property together. No one has his or her own land, business, or house; everyone owns everything together.

In governments that have been built on this idea, the state, or government, is said to own everything. The people have very little power or freedom because everything belongs to the state. The national leaders run everything and control the elections (if elections are held).

Communism is supposed to be a big group of people who govern themselves, but communist countries usually become dictatorships of the state. National leaders do whatever they want. The people themselves become servants of the leaders and have few rights or freedoms.

KEY VERSE: *When you want a certain piece of land, you find a way to seize it. When you want someone's house, you take it by fraud and violence. No one's family or inheritance is safe with you around! (Micah 2:2)*

RELATED VERSES: *Genesis 47:18-21; Acts 2:44*

RELATED QUESTIONS: *How come communism didn't like Christians and sent them to jail or to faraway places? What is the cause of communism falling?*

NOTE TO PARENTS: *Although some government systems are better than others, all have flaws. Only God's kingdom is perfect. Only God can rule perfectly because only God is completely unselfish, loves everyone, and always knows what is best.*

Q: WHY DO GOVERNMENTS DO WRONG THINGS?

144

A: Governments do wrong things for the same reason that individual persons do wrong things—sin. Every person is sinful. That means that people are naturally self-centered, and they try to live their lives without God. Some people are more sinful than others. That is, they work very hard to cheat, lie, and steal. Governments are made up of people, so they will sometimes do wrong things unless someone is keeping an eye on them and stops them. That is why many governments are organized with a system of "checks and balances," which lets one branch of government stop the actions of another. Democratic governments hold elections every few years. That gives the people the chance to get rid of bad leaders.

The good news is that God does not ignore the deeds of leaders. He watches over those who hold authority in government. Pray that God will make your country's leaders just and wise.

KEY VERSES: *I also noticed that throughout the world there is evil in the courtroom. Yes, even the courts of law are corrupt! I said to myself, "In due season God will judge everyone, both good and bad, for all their deeds." (Ecclesiastes 3:16-17)*

RELATED VERSES: *1 Kings 2:1-3; Psalms 53:3; 94:20-23; Romans 3:10; 1 Timothy 2:2*

Q: WHY DO GOVERNMENTS DO THINGS WRONG?

145

A:

Governments don't always do things wrong, even though people sometimes like to complain about the government. Government forms and programs can often be very complicated, and that's frustrating for a lot of people who have to deal with them. Of course, government leaders and officials will sometimes make mistakes and blunders. We all make mistakes. No government is perfect because no human being is perfect.

Although no government is perfect, people need government. If we didn't have leaders, laws, police officers, firefighters, tax collectors, and other government workers, every person would do whatever he or she wanted, and the country would be in a mess.

KEY VERSE: *Remind your people to submit to the government and its officers. They should be obedient, always ready to do what is good. (Titus 3:1)*

RELATED VERSE: *1 Timothy 2:2*

ENVIRONMENTAL
CONCERNS

Q: HOW MUCH DOES RECYCLING HELP?

146

A: It helps a lot. Recycling is important because people are using the natural resources of the earth very rapidly. For example, crude oil is used to heat homes and to make gasoline for cars and trucks. Many other products also come from oil, including plastics, tires, and jet fuel. Yet there is only so much oil in the earth. When it is used up, it will all be gone.

Recycling used oil, plastic, and rubber makes these resources stretch. We don't use up things so fast. And we are able to reuse the materials to make other things. God does not want us to be wasteful.

At the same time, we don't need to fear running out of the things we need. God created us. He created this earth. He put us on this earth to live and enjoy it. He provides the things we need. If we run out of oil, it will be OK, because God will still be in charge, and he will always provide the things we need.

So recycle and don't be wasteful, but don't be afraid of running out of things either. Just be a responsible user of the good things God lets you have and use.

KEY VERSE: *"Now gather the leftovers," Jesus told his disciples, "so that nothing is wasted." (John 6:12)*

RELATED VERSE: *Proverbs 12:27*

RELATED QUESTIONS: *Why do we have to drop things off at a recycling depot? How much garbage can recycling plants hold? What do they do with the garbage?*

NOTE TO PARENTS: *You may want to mention that garbage goes to landfills. Pretty soon all the landfills will be filled up with trash and garbage. Often the garbage pollutes our soil and water. We've used more nonrenewable resources since World War II than we used in all of history before. Recycling is simply a responsible way to live.*

Q: HOW CAN THEY RECYCLE MILK JUGS AFTER PEOPLE STEP ON THEM?

147

A: When items such as plastic milk jugs are recycled, they are combined with other plastic items, melted, and used to make other products. For example, recycled plastic bottles are often used to make playground equipment. Other kinds of bottles and containers are reused this way too. The bottles are *never* just washed out and refilled with milk. The government does not permit that because it would spread germs and disease. So stepping on empty milk jugs doesn't hurt in recycling.

KEY VERSES: *People know how to mine silver and refine gold. They know how to dig iron from the earth and smelt copper from stone. (Job 28:1-2)*

RELATED VERSE: *John 6:12*

RELATED QUESTIONS: *How do you recycle cans? When people recycle newspapers, how do they get the ink off?*

Q: WHY DO PEOPLE LITTER SO MUCH WHEN THEY CAN JUST THROW THEIR TRASH IN THE GARBAGE CAN?

148

A: Some people litter by accident. They are careless or do not pay attention to what happens to their food wrappers and other trash. People who litter on purpose, however, do so because they are not showing respect for other people or the earth.

We should pick up trash instead of littering or ignoring the litter on the ground. Just because we didn't drop it doesn't mean we should say, "It's not my mess." We are all keepers of God's earth. If everyone pitched in and picked up a little, the world would be a nicer, tidier place.

KEY VERSE: *The Lord God placed the man in the Garden of Eden to tend and care for it. (Genesis 2:15)*

RELATED VERSES: *Proverbs 18:9; 26:13; Romans 8:19-22*

RELATED QUESTIONS: *Why do people litter? If littering is against the law, just how important is this law?*

NOTE TO PARENTS: *Kids often object by saying, "But I didn't make the mess!" without realizing that their objection is irrelevant. We all live in a community, and we all share in the care of the environment. God's way is for us to look out for each other. Take your kids out with bags and gloves and clean up the litter at the school or the park and use the opportunity to teach these principles.*

Q: WHY DO PEOPLE WANT TO WRECK THE EARTH WITH POLLUTION?

149

A: Most people don't want to wreck the earth. Instead, people pollute because they don't think about the consequences of polluting or because they don't care about the damage it might do. Some may actually believe that littering and dumping waste really don't matter, that they don't hurt anything, or that it's someone else's job to clean it up.

Some people pollute because they are just too lazy to walk to a trash can. They are more concerned with doing things the easy way than with doing what is right.

KEY VERSE: *For we know that all creation has been groaning as in the pains of childbirth right up to the present time. (Romans 8:22)*

RELATED VERSES: *Proverbs 6:6-11; 20:4; Romans 8:19-21*

RELATED QUESTIONS: *Why do people pollute the world all the time? When they flatten the cars, does it pollute the air? Why are we ruining the earth if we only have one?*

NOTE TO PARENTS: *Whenever you answer a child's question about what others do wrong, be careful to guard against judging others. Help your child to focus on his or her own behavior and not judge others. God loves everyone, and we don't know why people do what they do. Pray together for the people you see doing wrong, that God will bless them with wisdom and truth.*

Q: WHY IS THERE SO MUCH POLLUTION IN THE CITIES?

150

A: The main reason there is so much pollution in the cities is that there are so many people. Lots of people means lots of cars, buses, trucks, restaurants, stores, industry, and garbage. In most cities with all the buildings and traffic, it can be difficult to clean up right away. Sometimes events in cities (such as parades, games, concerts, and rallies) attract lots of people who litter. If one person in a field throws a wrapper on the ground, it may not seem like a big deal. But if 100,000 people in the city each throw a wrapper on the ground, that's 100,000 wrappers!

All the traffic and factories add to air pollution and noise pollution, too. In smaller towns and out in the country, there aren't as many cars, trucks, buses, and people to contribute to the pollution problems.

KEY VERSE: *Upright citizens bless a city and make it prosper, but the talk of the wicked tears it apart. (Proverbs 11:11)*

RELATED VERSES: *Genesis 2:15; Proverbs 11:10; 14:4*

RELATED QUESTIONS: *If smog hurts people, why do people make smog out of factories? How do cars make so much smoke? Why do people live in this trash? Is there some kind of filter you can put on the smog? How does pollution kill us?*

Q: WHY DO SOME COMPANIES THROW DANGEROUS CHEMICALS INTO RIVERS AND OCEANS?

JASON'S IMAGINATION

151

A: It used to be that companies dumped a lot of chemicals into rivers and oceans because they didn't know that the chemicals were hurting anything. But when it was discovered how harmful some chemicals can be, the government made laws against dumping them. Now if companies pollute, they are disobeying the law. Sadly, some companies continue to dump dangerous chemicals into our waterways, even though they know they should dispose of them in safer ways. They do this because it's expensive to be careful and clean, and they don't want to spend the money.

KEY VERSE: *Those who love money will never have enough. How absurd to think that wealth brings true happiness! (Ecclesiastes 5:10)*

RELATED QUESTIONS: *Why do people throw chemicals into the water? When water gets dirty, how do they get it clean? Why would people want to kill fish just for a place to dump their waste? If people know chemicals are bad, why don't they dump them in space?*

NOTE TO PARENTS: *It is easy to pollute by disposing of chemicals improperly, because disposing of them properly can be time consuming and expensive. This is why many consumers routinely throw away oil, paint, and other chemicals in unsafe ways. Do your best to set a good example and dispose of these things as safely as possible, even if it is difficult or costs you money.*

Q: WHY DO PEOPLE LIVE ALL THEIR LIVES IN A CITY AND ONLY GO OUT INTO THE COUNTRYSIDE FOR PICNICS?

152

A: Most people live in cities because that's where their jobs are. People need jobs to make money so they can buy food, clothes, and everything else they need. And they know it's very convenient to live close to their job. So they live near their place of work. Many people also like the busyness and the many activities to choose from in the city.

The countryside is a nice change of pace. It is a lot calmer and more peaceful than the city, and there is much less pollution there. So people like to go there occasionally for vacations and picnics. It's a nice relaxing break from their normal routine.

KEY VERSE: *That night some shepherds were in the fields outside the village, guarding their flocks of sheep. (Luke 2:8)*

RELATED VERSES: *Psalm 19:1; Amos 9:14*

RELATED QUESTIONS: *How can people live that way? Why is it called Mother Nature instead of Father Nature? Where did the phrase "Mother Nature" come from?*

Q: WHY DO PEOPLE WANT TO CUT DOWN THE TREES?

153

A: People cut down trees

1. to make paper
2. to get wood for building houses, furniture, and other things
3. to clear land for new houses and buildings
4. to clear land for farms

It is all right to cut down trees because new trees can be planted in their place. We need paper for newspapers, magazines, and books, and paper is recyclable. We need wood for building. We need houses to live in. We need farmland to grow food.

This doesn't mean that people should cut down trees anywhere and anytime they feel like it. And they certainly shouldn't cut down trees just to be destructive. Trees provide beauty, shade, and places for birds to nest. Some trees provide flowers and fruit. And some trees help stop the wind; others help prevent soil erosion. We should take care of the trees we have.

KEY VERSE: *Joshua replied, "If the hill country of Ephraim is not large enough for you, clear out land for yourselves in the forest where the Perizzites and Rephaites live." (Joshua 17:15)*

RELATED VERSES: *Genesis 6:14; 22:3; Exodus 37:1; 1 Kings 5:1-10*

RELATED QUESTIONS: *If there are lots of trees in the world, why don't people set aside certain trees to be cut down? Why do the woodcutters destroy God's world?*

Q: WHAT CAN CHILDREN DO TO HELP TAKE BETTER CARE OF THE WORLD?

154

A: Sometimes it seems as though children can't do very much to make a difference in the world. After all, adults own the factories, stores, and restaurants and drive the trucks, buses, and cars. But children can help a lot. Here are a few ideas to get you started:

1. Do not litter; throw your trash away instead of throwing it on the ground.
2. Recycle paper, plastic, glass, oil, and anything else that can be recycled.
3. Take good care of your pets; they are part of God's world too.
4. Don't waste food; take only as much as you can eat.
5. Don't waste water; turn off the faucet when you're done using it.
6. Don't waste electricity; turn off the lights when you don't need them.
7. Live simply; be content with things that are a little less expensive or fancy instead of insisting on new toys or clothes.

KEY VERSE: *You put us in charge of everything you made, giving us authority over all things. (Psalm 8:6)*

RELATED VERSES: *Genesis 1:28-31; Proverbs 12:10; 24:30-34; John 6:12*

RELATED QUESTIONS: *Why doesn't everybody participate in making a better place to live? Why don't people try to save our world? Why are we waiting to take better care of our world?*

ANIMALS

Q: WHY ARE ANIMALS BECOMING EXTINCT ALL OVER THE WORLD?

A: The biggest reason some animals are becoming extinct is disruption of habitat. People move in and take away the land used by the animals. Some people don't seem to care what happens to the plants and animals of the earth. They just do whatever they want, regardless of the consequences to nature. But God has given human beings the job of taking care of the world. That means taking good care of *all* of it, animals included.

Remember that this all starts with you. Take good care of your pets, don't litter so they have a clean place to live, and take good care of God's earth. After all, it all belongs to God, and we are his stewards.

KEY VERSE: *For all the animals of the forest are mine, and I own the cattle on a thousand hills. (Psalm 50:10)*

RELATED VERSES: *Genesis 1:28-31; Proverbs 12:10; Ezekiel 34:25*

RELATED QUESTIONS: *Should we stop killing animals? Should we pray for endangered animals?*

156

A: When sin entered the world, all of creation was damaged. Ever since that time, pain and suffering have been a part of life. People and animals suffer—no one escapes.

Probably the greatest danger to animals is other animals that attack and kill them for food. Animals eat each other because they are part of the food chain. They need the food to survive. Some animals eat only plants, but many eat other animals. For example, dragonflies eat mosquitoes, birds eat worms and other insects, cats eat mice and birds, and some big fish eat baby ducks. Some animals, called scavengers, eat dead animals that they find in the woods or along the highway. God created animals that way. If all the animals continued to live, soon the world would be filled with them.

KEY VERSES: *You send the darkness, and it becomes night, when all the forest animals prowl about. Then the young lions roar for their food, but they are dependent on God. (Psalm 104:20-21)*

RELATED VERSES: *Genesis 3:14-19; Job 39:13-18, 26-30; Ecclesiastes 10:8-9; Isaiah 11:6; Matthew 10:29*

Q: WHY DO PEOPLE KILL ANIMALS TO EAT WHEN THEY COULD JUST BUY FOOD AT THE STORE?

157

A: Many years ago, everyone had to hunt for food. They would gather plants and kill animals. Then some people began to raise fruits and vegetables and sell them. Others raised animals and sold them. Eventually, there were grocery stores where people could buy the fruit, vegetables, milk, and meat they needed to eat. But for meat to be available at a store, someone has to kill the animals.

It certainly is more convenient to buy meat at a store than to raise chickens or hunt wild pigs. But some people enjoy hunting, so they hunt deer, moose, pheasant, or some other animal instead of buying all their meat at the store.

No matter where we get our food, we should always thank God for it. The food we have is part of what God provides for us so we can live.

KEY VERSES: *God blessed Noah and his sons and told them, "Multiply and fill the earth. All the wild animals, large and small, and all the birds and fish will be afraid of you. I have placed them in your power. I have given them to you for food, just as I have given you grain and vegetables." (Genesis 9:1-3)*

RELATED VERSES: *Acts 10:9-13; 1 Corinthians 10:30-31*

RELATED QUESTIONS: *Why do people think we shouldn't eat animals or meat? Why do people think we shouldn't eat animals even if they're raised for it?*

Q: WHY ARE SOME PEOPLE MEAN TO ANIMALS?

158

A: Some people who don't care about animals are mean to them for fun. Other people hurt animals without meaning to when they are angry or frustrated. For example, someone might be having a very bad day. Then, when this person comes home and the pet has done something annoying, the person takes out his or her anger on the pet. We don't always know why other people are mean, but we can ask God to help us be kind and not mean. He can help us take good care of his creation.

KEY VERSE: *The godly are concerned for the welfare of their animals, but even the kindness of the wicked is cruel. (Proverbs 12:10)*

RELATED VERSES: *Proverbs 16:32; Colossians 3:12*

RELATED QUESTIONS: *Why do people sometimes try to hurt harmless animals? Why are people mean to God's creatures? Why do we kill animals even though they do no harm?*

Q: DO ANIMALS HAVE FEELINGS JUST LIKE PEOPLE DO?

159

A: Animals have feelings, but they are not exactly like people. Think about your body. Animals have bodies just as we have bodies, but they're not the same kind of bodies. Humans have a unique brain structure. They can think about the future. A dog will bury a bone, but she won't sit on the porch and wonder if she has buried enough bones for retirement. It is a lot like that with feelings. A dog can feel lonely, sad, afraid, and hungry. But the dog cannot think about the reasons for those feelings. The dog only responds to certain conditions (for example, he feels alone and sad in a kennel or afraid when the thunder roars and the lightning cracks). God has given us more complex emotions that we can experience, enjoy, use, and direct.

KEY VERSE: *Do you think we are cattle? Do you think we have no intelligence? (Job 18:3)*

RELATED VERSE: *Proverbs 26:11*

RELATED QUESTIONS: *Do animals have feelings like we do? Why can't animals have feelings?*

Q: WHY DO PEOPLE CRY WHEN THEIR PETS DIE?

160

A: Every good thing that we enjoy is a gift from God. Many people often enjoy their pets and like having them around. They grow very attached to a favorite pet. Animals are loyal, they appreciate their masters, and after they are trained, they don't give their masters much grief. Many people come to like their pets very much. Some people treat their pets as though they are members of the family. So when a pet gets lost or dies, the master feels very sad and may even cry. It is OK to cry when you lose a pet that you loved.

KEY VERSES: *If you had one hundred sheep, and one of them strayed away and was lost in the wilderness, wouldn't you leave the ninety-nine others to go and search for the lost one until you found it? And then you would joyfully carry it home on your shoulders. When you arrived, you would call together your friends and neighbors to rejoice with you because your lost sheep was found. (Luke 15:4-6)*

RELATED VERSE: *1 Timothy 6:17*

RELATED QUESTION: *Why shouldn't people cry when their pet dies? The pet is sort of like family.*

Q: WHY DO SOME ANIMALS LOOK FUNNY?

161

A: God is very creative. He made a huge variety of plants and animals—hundreds of thousands of kinds. And remember that *every person* is special and different. This variety is part of God's creative genius. It is part of the beauty he built into the world.

Some animals look funny because they are built a certain way to help them live in their environment and to get food. An armadillo, for example, has a hard shell that protects it from other animals. A lizard has a long, sticky tongue to help it catch flies to eat. An anteater has a long nose to help it eat ants. The giraffe's long neck helps it eat leaves from tall trees. God made all animals with amazing mechanisms for survival, and that's just one of the wonders of God himself.

KEY VERSES: *Take a look at the mighty hippopotamus. I made it, just as I made you. It eats grass like an ox. See its powerful loins and the muscles of its belly. Its tail is as straight as a cedar. The sinews of its thighs are tightly knit together. Its bones are tubes of bronze. Its limbs are bars of iron. It is a prime example of God's amazing handiwork. Only its Creator can threaten it. (Job 40:15-19)*

RELATED VERSES: *Genesis 1:20-25; Psalm 19:1*

RELATED QUESTION: *Why were animals made?*

NOTE TO PARENTS: *Encourage your children with the fact that God created them to be wonderfully unique.*

Q: WHY DO CATS AND DOGS FIGHT?

162

A: Usually cats and dogs fight because they are trying to protect their territory. It is natural for animals to compete for dominance (to see who is the strongest). Dogs and cats that are raised with each other usually don't fight. They are used to each other and get along pretty well.

KEY VERSES: *In that day the wolf and the lamb will live together; the leopard and the goat will be at peace. Calves and yearlings will be safe among lions, and a little child will lead them all. The cattle will graze among bears. Cubs and calves will lie down together. And lions will eat grass as the livestock do. (Isaiah 11:6-7)*

RELATED QUESTIONS: *Why do animals fight each other? Why do cats chase after rats? Why do dogs chase cats? Why does my cat chase and fight my neighbor's big fat cat? How come guinea pigs fight other guinea pigs? How come crabs fight other crabs? How come fighting fish fight with other fighting fish?*

THE
ENTERTAINMENT
INDUSTRY

Q: WHY DO MOVIES HAVE WEIRDOS FOR STARS?

HOLLYWOOD MAKE-UP STUDIO

163

A: Not all movie stars are weirdos. Many are normal people who live pretty normal lives. The news media don't report these normal lives. They report the abnormal ones—the weird cases. So we hear a lot about the weirdos and nothing about the rest of the normal stars. That makes it seem as though all of the movie and television actors are weird, but they're not.

Some stars act weird on purpose in order to get attention. In other words, they put on an act so newspaper and magazine stories will be written about them. They think this will help their career.

Others act weird because they have an exaggerated idea of their own importance. Because so many people tell them how great they are and because they get a lot of attention and money for doing their job, they sometimes think they can do anything they want. So they take drugs, trash hotel rooms, marry and divorce several times, and do other shocking things. The sin of pride can make people do strange things.

KEY VERSES: *Everything they do is for show. . . . They enjoy the attention they get on the streets. (Matthew 23:5, 7)*

RELATED VERSES: *Psalm 49:16-18; Proverbs 11:2; 12:23; 16:8, 27; Matthew 23:5-12; Luke 6:24-26*

RELATED QUESTION: *Why does Hollywood make movies?*

NOTE TO PARENTS: *Children often idolize movie stars and athletes for the wrong reasons. Help your children understand the difference between liking a person's skills and wanting to be like that person. We should strive to be like people who are wise and good, not like those who are popular.*

164

A: Junk entertainment is like junk food—it tastes good even though it's bad for us. Many people watch garbage on TV and in the movies because they like it, even though it is bad for them.

God wants us to be *discerning*. He wants us to recognize junk entertainment for what it is and avoid it, even if it seems fun or harmless. Ratings help many people decide whether or not to see certain movies or TV shows. A movie rated G is said to be all right for "General Audiences." In other words, people of all ages will probably not be offended or hurt by anything in the movie.

The ratings are not always right, however. That's why it is helpful to read reviews or talk with others about a movie or TV show. Some movies can have a mild rating (for example, G or PG) and yet teach some pretty bad stuff about God and life.

Be careful about what you watch because once you've watched something, you can't unwatch it.

KEY VERSE: *Fix your thoughts on what is true and honorable and right. Think about things that are pure and lovely and admirable. Think about things that are excellent and worthy of praise. (Philippians 4:8)*

RELATED VERSES: *Deuteronomy 7:26; Psalms 101:3; 106:35-36; James 1:5-8*

RELATED QUESTIONS: *How come parents don't want us to watch bad shows and movies? If some movies are so bad, why are they fun to watch?*

NOTE TO PARENTS: *What you model is what your children will become. Choose entertainment wisely; think critically about the shows and movies you consider watching.*

Q: WHY IS THERE SO MUCH FIGHTING ON TV?

165

A: One reason is that there is so much fighting in real life. Some people have not learned to control their temper, so there is a lot of fighting. God wants us to overlook insults and stay calm when people try to make us mad. Too many people think they have no choice but to blow their top.

Another reason TV has a lot of fighting is that many people like to see other people fight. A lot of people watch shows with fighting in them, so the studios produce them and the networks show them. The TV and studio bosses often say they show fighting because it is an important part of the story and they have to be realistic. That may be true, but the real reason is money.

KEY VERSE: *Good people enjoy the positive results of their words, but those who are treacherous crave violence. (Proverbs 13:2)*

RELATED VERSES: *Genesis 6:5-6; Proverbs 20:3; 26:21*

RELATED QUESTIONS: *How can people make movies and shows about fighting and hurting and shooting each other? Why do we enjoy seeing other people get hurt?*

Q: HOW COME PEOPLE PUT BAD MOVIES ON TV?

166

A: Because lots of people watch them. The moviemakers and the network bosses try to make as much money as possible. If a lot of people watch a certain movie, the television network can make a lot of money through advertising. The networks know that lots of people watch bad shows. Instead of watching bad movies, we should ignore them by changing channels or turning off the TV set. If a lot of people wrote the TV stations and complained about the bad movies, maybe the networks wouldn't show them anymore.

Remember that bad is bad no matter how many people do it. You don't have to watch bad movies just because they're popular.

KEY VERSES: *Stop loving this evil world and all that it offers you, for when you love the world, you show that you do not have the love of the Father in you. For the world offers only the lust for physical pleasure, the lust for everything we see, and pride in our possessions. These are not from the Father. They are from this evil world. (1 John 2:15-16)*

RELATED VERSES: *Psalm 101:3; Philippians 4:8*

RELATED QUESTIONS: *What in the world is a V chip? Who invented the V chip? Why do the fighting video games make people want to fight?*

NOTE TO PARENTS: *Telling children they can't watch something "because it's bad" will arouse their curiosity and often backfire. Instead, tell your children what's in the show and why it's bad, or how it will adversely affect them. This will allow them to share in the decision, or at least to see that you have good reasons for it.*

Q: WHY DO MOVIE COMPANIES MAKE SCARY MOVIES IF THEY KNOW PEOPLE WILL HAVE NIGHTMARES?

167

A: Many people want to see scary movies and will pay money to see them. The companies that make these movies don't care about whether or not they are scary or bad. They just want to make money.

God doesn't want us to be afraid of monsters, demons, ghosts, and prowlers. He wants us to think good thoughts and be confident in his care for us, because he loves us and created us to enjoy life. So if something you're watching scares you, stop watching it. And if you see something that bothers you, talk to your parents about it and pray together that God will protect you and give you good dreams. God does not want you to have nightmares.

KEY VERSE: *I will lie down in peace and sleep, for you alone, O Lord, will keep me safe. (Psalm 4:8)*

RELATED VERSES: *Psalm 101:3; Romans 8:38-39*

RELATED QUESTIONS: *Why do people scare others with scary movies? Why does God let Satan scare us with scary movies? Why isn't there just a certain channel for horror shows? Why do they put kids in horror movies, then rate them R? Why do people make bad movies? Why do people make movies if they put fighting and violence in them?*

Q: WHY ARE SOME THINGS ON VIDEOS FUNNY FOR ADULTS BUT NOT FOR KIDS?

168

A: Some jokes are funny for adults but not for children because kids and adults have different kinds of humor. Each group finds different things funny. Also, adults have experiences that kids haven't had. They laugh at things that they know about. For example, a joke about working on the job, paying income tax, or raising children wouldn't be very funny to children. Only people who know about those situations would get the joke.

A good family movie will often include humor for the kids and for the adults so the whole family can enjoy it together.

KEY VERSE: *It's like this: When I was a child, I spoke and thought and reasoned as a child does. But when I grew up, I put away childish things. (1 Corinthians 13:11)*

RELATED QUESTION: *Why do people laugh at jokes that aren't funny?*

NOTE TO PARENTS: *Humor and laughter are gifts from God. If your children have a great sense of humor and can readily make others laugh, encourage them to use the gift wisely and not to abuse it with cruelty or offensive language.*

Q: WHY WON'T PARENTS LET KIDS WATCH CERTAIN SHOWS THE KIDS WANT TO WATCH?

169

A: Because God gives parents the responsibility to guide their children, and sometimes parents know something about a show that the kids don't know. Parents know that the show will have violence or swearing or will make bad things look good. They may not let their children watch those kinds of shows. Most parents also know that too much TV is not good. Good parents put limits on how much television and what shows their family can watch.

KEY VERSE: *Children, obey your parents because you belong to the Lord, for this is the right thing to do. (Ephesians 6:1)*

RELATED VERSES: *Psalm 101:3; Proverbs 4:23*

RELATED QUESTIONS: *If you get cable and there's a channel with all bad shows, why don't your parents phone and ask the cable company to take that off their bill? Why do people make bad shows in the first place? Why do people like TV with so many channels?*

Q: WHY DO PEOPLE LIKE DIFFERENT KINDS OF MUSIC?

170

A: People like various kinds of music because people have different tastes. Each person is unique and special—a part of the variety in God's creation. It's the same with people's tastes in food. Everyone has favorite foods. We wouldn't expect everyone to eat and like all the same foods.

Certain groups of people like certain kinds of music. People of one nationality may like one kind, and people from one area of the country may have their own musical likes and dislikes. Some people just listen to whatever is popular.

We should choose music (and other forms of entertainment) wisely, because it's something we put into our mind. God wants us to think about good things.

KEY VERSE: *Just as the mouth tastes good food, the ear tests the words it hears. (Job 34:3)*

RELATED VERSES: *Judges 5:3; Psalm 81:1-3; Proverbs 4:23; Ephesians 5:19*

RELATED QUESTIONS: *Why does God let you rot your brain with bad music? Why does God let people sing bad music? Who invented music? How come music gets so loud? How many types of music are there? How many songs are there in the world? How can people listen to rock music?*

Q: WHY ARE MUSICIANS TREATED LIKE IDOLS?

171

A: Everybody looks up to somebody. God made us this way so we could learn and grow into people who love and obey him. He gives us parents to start the process, and as we get older we choose others from whom to learn.

Many people choose to idolize musicians because they appear in the spotlight a lot. They are featured in newspapers and magazines and on TV and are held up as heroes. Many people look up to them simply because of all the attention they get.

Others "worship" musicians because their music makes them feel something very deeply. That is the way art works—it touches people's emotions.

And others idolize musicians because they assume that being rich and famous is important. Not all musicians are rich and famous, but those who are may appear to be especially successful or great.

KEY VERSE: *Friends, why are you doing this? We are merely human beings like yourselves! We have come to bring you the Good News that you should turn from these worthless things to the living God, who made heaven and earth, the sea, and everything in them. (Acts 14:15)*

RELATED VERSES: *Acts 14:11-18*

NOTE TO PARENTS: *We should choose our heroes carefully, and we should be careful not to idolize them. Encourage your children to look up to those who love God and try to do what is right. Help them to realize that no one is perfect, not even great heroes.*

Q: WHY ARE THERE COMMERCIALS ALL THE TIME WHEN GOOD SHOWS ARE ON TV?

172

A: The commercials pay for the shows. That is, the companies that show the programs get paid by the companies that make the commercials. If the networks did not show the commercials, they would have no money to pay for the programs. A lot of people watch the very popular shows, so that is why you see so many commercials. The companies advertising want to show their commercials when a lot of people are watching.

KEY VERSE: *Do not cheat or rob anyone. Always pay your hired workers promptly. (Leviticus 19:13)*

RELATED VERSE: *Proverbs 11:26*

RELATED QUESTIONS: *Why are there commercials? Why are there commercials on TV and not in movies? Why do they show previews of movies? Why not just make it a surprise?*

Q:

WHEN YOU WANT TO HAVE SOMETHING YOU SEE ON A TV COMMERCIAL, WHY DOESN'T YOUR MOM LET YOU HAVE IT?

173

A: Many times the products advertised on television look much better than they really are, and your parents know it. Your parents have the responsibility to guide and protect you. Their job is to teach you God's ways and God's wisdom. They may not let you have something that looks exciting on TV because they know that it isn't going to be as great as the commercial shows. Or they may know that you do not need it or that it costs too much money. Or they know that it would actually be bad for you, even if you can't imagine how.

KEY VERSE: *Then he said, "Beware! Don't be greedy for what you don't have. Real life is not measured by how much we own." (Luke 12:15)*

RELATED VERSES: *Ephesians 6:1-3; 1 John 2:15-17*

RELATED QUESTIONS: *When you get something you saw on a commercial, why don't you like it? Why do commercials have to say, "It's not available at stores"?*

FAMILY
MATTERS

174

A: God's plan is for a husband and wife to stay together and not get divorced. But all people have weaknesses. No one is perfect. That is why troubles arise in all relationships, even between two people who love each other very much.

When a man and a woman get married, they promise to stay with each other for life. They know it won't always be easy, but they want to work out their problems and stay together. When the arguments and other conflicts and pressures come, some people don't know how to handle them, and their problems get worse. Usually the problems start small and then grow. Eventually, these problems can become so big that the husband or the wife or both just give up and decide to end their marriage. Some don't try that hard; they divorce because they choose not to work out their problems.

But God wants Christians to stay married and work things out. He knows that when they do, their lives will be better for it.

KEY VERSES: *Jesus replied, "Moses permitted divorce as a concession to your hard-hearted wickedness, but it was not what God had originally intended. And I tell you this, a man who divorces his wife and marries another commits adultery—unless his wife has been unfaithful." (Matthew 19:8-9)*

RELATED VERSES: *Proverbs 18:22; Matthew 19:3-12; Romans 3:23; 1 Corinthians 7:10-11, 26-28*

RELATED QUESTIONS: *Why do people marry if they're just going to get divorced? Why do some people just get married without having a ceremony? What is the youngest kids can get married?*

175

A: Most fights between brothers and sisters are normal. When you live with somebody, sometimes you get annoyed with each other, or you both try to use the same thing, or you both want to occupy the same space, or you each want to do things differently. This happens in every family—even in families where people love each other very much.

The next time you disagree with your brother or sister, here's what to do. Try to state your differences without yelling or hitting. If you are upset, calm down and lower your voice. Tell the person how you feel. It also helps to try to see things from the other person's point of view. Listen to each other without interrupting. Then as you talk it out, you can suggest a way to solve the problem. Maybe you can take turns. Maybe you can give up a little of what you wanted. Remember that you're both on the same team.

Every conflict is an opportunity for you to learn one of life's most valuable skills—how to get along with others. It will not happen by magic. You have to learn how to do it, like learning how to ride a bike. It takes work, prayer, and practice.

KEY VERSES: *Never pay back evil for evil to anyone. Do things in such a way that everyone can see you are honorable. Do your part to live in peace with everyone, as much as possible. (Romans 12:17-18)*

RELATED VERSES: *Proverbs 15:1; 17:9, 13, 27; 20:22; 26:21; Romans 12:10; Ephesians 4:32; 1 John 3:11-12*

RELATED QUESTIONS: *Brothers and sisters are supposed to be nice to each other, but how come they always fight? Why don't brothers and sisters get along? Why can't sisters be more supportive?*

Q: WHY DO SOME KIDS HAVE STEPMOTHERS OR STEPFATHERS?

STEP DAD   ROPE DAD

176

A: Stepmothers and stepfathers come into the picture whenever a parent remarries. That is, one of the parents dies or divorces the other. If the other parent gets married again, the children get a new mother or father. This person is called a *stepmother* or *stepfather*.

For example, suppose a boy's mother and father get divorced and the boy lives with his mother. If the mother remarries, her new husband becomes the boy's stepfather. Or suppose a girl's mother dies. If the girl's father remarries, his new wife becomes the girl's stepmother. If the stepfather or stepmother brings children into the family, the children of the two families become stepbrothers and stepsisters. And if the newly married parents have more children after they get married, those children become half brothers and half sisters of the children that came before them.

Divorce and remarriage can be confusing. But remember that no matter what label we give to the parents and kids in a family, they are still all part of one family. It doesn't matter how they came together.

KEY VERSE: *A wife is married to her husband as long as he lives. If her husband dies, she is free to marry whomever she wishes, but this must be a marriage acceptable to the Lord. (1 Corinthians 7:39)*

RELATED VERSES: *Matthew 19:3-12; 1 Corinthians 7:1-40*

RELATED QUESTIONS: *What are half brothers and half sisters? Why do parents sometimes not like their children?*

177

A: One reason parents used to have more kids is that before modern medicine, more children died young, from disease and other problems, than die today. Parents could not be sure that their children would live. Another reason families of the past had a lot of children is that they needed many family members to help with the family work—around the house or on the farm. Modern medicine has also made it easier than ever to prevent pregnancy.

God loves families of all shapes and sizes. Today, some families do have a lot of children. But it is not as common as it used to be.

KEY VERSE: *God blessed them and told them, "Multiply and fill the earth and subdue it. Be masters over the fish and birds and all the animals." (Genesis 1:28)*

RELATED VERSES: *Genesis 17:6; 42:32; Psalm 127:3-5*

Q: HOW ARE FAMILIES DIFFERENT NOW FROM THE WAY THEY USED TO BE?

178

A: In some ways families are very different. Before cars and planes were invented, families were very close and lots of relatives lived together. Most families were also larger, with more children. New inventions have caused many families to spread far apart. Now people can travel long distances very quickly by car, airplane, bus, boat, or train to visit family, and they can communicate with each other on the phone and through electronic mail.

But in many ways families are still the same. Families start with a mom and a dad. The parents have parents. Kids have grandparents. And sometimes the grandparents or other relatives live with the family.

KEY VERSES: *The church should care for any widow who has no one else to care for her. But if she has children or grandchildren, their first responsibility is to show godliness at home and repay their parents by taking care of them. This is something that pleases God very much. (1 Timothy 5:3-4)*

RELATED VERSES: *Acts 16:33-34; 1 Timothy 3:4-5; 5:8; 2 Timothy 1:5*

RELATED QUESTION: *How come families changed?*

CHANGING TECHNOLOGY

Q: HOW FAST IS TECHNOLOGY CHANGING?

"NEW COMPUTERS" &
DAY-OLD COMPUTERS
SOLD HERE

179

A: Technology is changing very fast. Just think of some of the things that people use every day:

- Television was invented in 1926.
- Penicillin was first used to cure disease in 1929.
- The microwave oven was invented in 1947.
- The VCR was invented in 1965.
- The personal computer was invented in 1972.
- Cellular phones were first used by the public in 1979.
- The World Wide Web was created in 1990.

These recent inventions have become very important to us. And right now, as you are reading this, people are inventing new machines, medicines, appliances, computers, and other technologies that can help us even more. This all comes from the creativity God gave us.

KEY VERSE: *And people should eat and drink and enjoy the fruits of their labor, for these are gifts from God. (Ecclesiastes 3:13)*

RELATED VERSES: *Proverbs 25:2; Ecclesiastes 1:9-10; 3:1-15*

RELATED QUESTIONS: *What in technology is changing? What is technology?*

Q: HOW DID COMPUTERS GET SO SMART?

180

A: Computers do not think, so they aren't smart in the way that human beings are smart. Computers simply process information very, very fast. They receive and send electrical signals according to a set of rules, called instructions, built into the main chip. The computers of today seem "smarter" than older ones because they run much faster, and because they have more instructions built into them. But they still just process information according to a set of rules.

Some people think that human beings are very special computers, with the "main chip" in their head. But this is not true. A person is much more than just a brain, and a brain is much more than a big computer chip. A person is a combination of body, soul, and spirit. A person is created in the image of God. Computers are just machines. They aren't anything like "smart."

KEY VERSE: *For the Lord grants wisdom! From his mouth come knowledge and understanding. (Proverbs 2:6)*

RELATED VERSES: *Genesis 1:27; Psalms 8:5; 139:13-16; Jeremiah 9:23-24*

RELATED QUESTIONS: *How come people think computers will take over the world? Why do we need computers? Who invented computers?*

181

A: A computer virus is a program that copies itself to another computer by attaching itself to programs or data. Computers get viruses when people load or run infected files on their computers. They are called viruses because they work like living viruses—by making copies of themselves and attaching themselves to, or "infecting," another machine. Most do this when someone opens or runs an infected file on their own computer.

Viruses don't just arise out of nowhere. People write them. Some of those who write viruses claim that it's not their fault if users get infected files. But that is just an example of how sin and selfishness can blind us to the truth. God says we should look out for each other, respect each other, and love each other, because everything we do affects someone else. It is true that most viruses do not cause any damage or harm. But some are written to cause mischief or damage to data. And even the harmless ones take time and energy to get rid of. Damaging someone else's property is wrong.

KEY VERSES: *Just as damaging as a mad man shooting a lethal weapon is someone who lies to a friend and then says, "I was only joking." (Proverbs 26:18-19)*

RELATED VERSES: *Proverbs 2:12-14; Luke 6:31*

Q: HOW COME THE KEYS ON THE KEYBOARD ARE NOT IN ALPHABETICAL ORDER?

182

A: Computer keyboards made today have the same layout as the very first typewriter ever made. The typewriter was invented by Christopher Sholes of Milwaukee, Wisconsin, in 1867. The layout for the keys he came up with is called a QWERTY layout because those letters are the first six letters on the top row. Sholes chose this layout because he believed it would be easy to use—the placement of the letters would make it easy to type English words quickly without jamming the parts of the typewriter. Typewriters and computer keyboards of today don't have any parts that can jam, but everyone is so used to using the QWERTY layout that we keep using it.

KEY VERSE: *Any story sounds true until someone sets the record straight. (Proverbs 18:17)*

Q: WHY DO PEOPLE SURF ON THE INTERNET?

183

A: People "surf" the Internet for many reasons:

- Curiosity—it can be interesting; they want to see what's there.
- Education—it can be informative; they want to answer questions or learn something.
- Information—it can tell them something they need to know, such as a weather forecast, a sports schedule, or the route to a place.
- Entertainment—it can be fun; they want to listen to music, meet people, read interesting stories, or see video clips.
- Problem solving—it can help them find answers to a problem they have.
- Communication—it can be a way to send and receive messages.

KEY VERSE: *Wise people treasure knowledge, but the babbling of a fool invites trouble. (Proverbs 10:14)*

RELATED VERSES: *Proverbs 15:14; 18:15; 27:20; Ecclesiastes 12:12; 1 John 2:16*

RELATED QUESTIONS: *Why do people get on the Internet? What does it mean to "surf" with a computer?*

Q: IS THE INTERNET BAD?

WELCOME
TO
HEDGEHOG
.COM

184

A: The Internet itself is not bad. It is just like any other tool, such as a hammer, a book, or a phone—it can be used for both good and bad. Almost anything can be used this way, even things that are usually used for good. A hammer can be used to build a house or hurt someone. So the Internet can be misused and used for bad purposes, just as it can be used for good purposes. Sadly, some people do use it the bad way.

By itself, the Internet is just a very big network of networks. Whether it is used for good or for bad is up to us. It has great potential for good. We each need to do our part and use it right—to the glory of God.

KEY VERSE: *Whatever you eat or drink or whatever you do, you must do all for the glory of God. (1 Corinthians 10:31)*

RELATED VERSES: *1 Corinthians 10:30-33*

RELATED QUESTIONS: *Who invented the Internet? Why are there bad pictures on the Internet? What are tele-communications? How much does the Internet cost?*

Q: HOW COME THE OLDEN DAYS AND THESE DAYS ARE DIFFERENT?

185

A: First, people change the way they dress, the style of their homes, and the kinds of foods they eat. Second, and more importantly, technology keeps changing. Every year, engineers and inventors create new products and new ways of doing things. Some of these things can improve our lives, and others make things a little harder, but all of them bring change.

After the automobile was invented and became common, people didn't have to ride horses or horse-drawn buggies to travel from town to town. That was a huge change. And just think of the changes that came from airplanes, telephones, microwave ovens, antibiotics, vaccines, and computers. Then microphones, televisions, tape players, CD players, VCRs, and CD-ROM drives sure changed entertainment. Not that long ago, people didn't have any of these inventions.

But even with all the changes, many things stay the same. Human nature is the same—people still struggle and search for God. People still laugh and cry, and are born young and grow old. A year is still 365 days, people still have to work, and each person still needs God's love and lordship. And everyone still dies.

KEY VERSE: *Don't long for "the good old days," for you don't know whether they were any better than today.* *(Ecclesiastes 7:10)*

RELATED QUESTIONS: *In olden days, did they have phones? How come TV used to be black and white? Who invented electricity? Who invented TV? What is satellite TV?*

MEDICINE

Q: WHY DO PEOPLE GET SICK WHEN GOD IS WATCHING OVER THEM?

186

A: Sickness was not part of God's original plan for us. We have sickness in the world because sin brought it in. As long as we live in this world, we will have sickness. God does not promise that he will keep all pain and sickness away from us, although he does promise to always be with us.

We need to take care of ourselves and guard against sickness by eating the right foods, getting enough sleep, and exercising. When we do get sick, we should take our medicine exactly as the doctor says and pray and ask God to help us recover.

Ecclesiastes 7:14 says, "Enjoy prosperity while you can. But when hard times strike, realize that both come from God."

In heaven God will end all sickness. This life is not all there is. Don't forget about heaven.

KEY VERSE: *Our bodies now disappoint us, but when they are raised, they will be full of glory. They are weak now, but when they are raised, they will be full of power. (1 Corinthians 15:43)*

RELATED VERSES: *Psalm 41:3; Romans 8:18-25; 2 Corinthians 12:8-10; James 5:14-15; Revelation 21:4*

RELATED QUESTIONS: *If God is watching over you, why do you still get the flu? How do you get diabetes? How do people get cancer? How does cancer start? How does asthma start? How do appendixes bust? How do you get constipated?*

Q: WHY DOES YOUR BODY FEEL SICK?

UNDER REPAIR: APPROACH WITH CAUTION!

187

A: When a person feels sick, that person's body is telling him or her that something is wrong. Pain and sick feelings can be a friend, an alarm system that alerts us to problems. Without these feelings, we would not know that something is wrong and that we need to do something about it (for example, eat certain foods, take medicine, or have an operation). People who don't have those bad feelings can hurt themselves more by not taking care of the problem.

KEY VERSES: *You guided my conception and formed me in the womb. You clothed me with skin and flesh, and you knit my bones and sinews together. (Job 10:10-11)*

RELATED VERSES: *Psalm 25:16-18; Revelation 21:4*

RELATED QUESTIONS: *How does your body feel that it's sick? How does your body get sick? Why do you get airsick?*

Q: WHAT ARE BACTERIA AND VIRUSES?

COSTUME PARTY

BACTERIA

VIRUS

188

A: Bacteria are one-celled living things; viruses are parasites that attack living things. Both are so small that you need a microscope to see them. Harmful bacteria and viruses are often called germs. Germs make you sick by reproducing inside your body.

Bacteria are not always harmful. E. coli bacteria live in your intestines and help your body break down food. Several kinds of bacteria live in the ground and break up dead leaves, sticks, grass, and other organic matter to make compost. These bacteria could make you sick if they got on your food, but they serve a good purpose in nature.

Other bacteria are very harmful; streptococcus bacteria, for example, cause strep throat, a sickness that children and adults sometimes get. Doctors treat it with antibiotics, medicines that kill bacteria.

Bacteria and viruses are everywhere, but God made our bodies to fight them off. He gave us white blood cells and antibodies. These are your body's way of staying well and of curing itself of sickness.

KEY VERSE: *Thank you for making me so wonderfully complex! Your workmanship is marvelous—and how well I know it. (Psalm 139:14)*

RELATED VERSES: *James 5:14-15*

RELATED QUESTIONS: *What are viruses? How do you get viruses? Why do people spread germs so fast and why are they so rude about it?*

Q: WHY DO DOCTORS GIVE SOME SHOTS THAT ARE LONG AND SOME THAT ARE SHORT?

189

A: Doctors give different kinds of shots for different reasons. If the doctor uses a long needle, it is because he or she needs to get the medicine deep into your body so it can do its work. Doctors are trained to know what kind of shots to give. It's a matter of using the treatment that fits what you need. God grants doctors the wisdom they need to treat their patients with skill.

Of course, doctors don't know everything, but God does. You can ask him to give your doctor wisdom and help him or her to do an even better job.

KEY VERSE: *Wounds from a friend are better than many kisses from an enemy. (Proverbs 27:6)*

RELATED VERSES: *Proverbs 17:22; Matthew 9:12; James 5:14-15*

RELATED QUESTIONS: *Why do we have to have needles for shots? How come you get measles shots and booster shots? Why do you get a shot before you get a cast?*

NOTE TO PARENTS: *You can pray with your children before going to the doctor to help teach them that we still depend on God for our health. The Designer and Manufacturer knows more than the repair person, and he wants us to come to him with our needs.*

Q: WHY ARE DOCTORS SO SMART?

190

A: God makes every person with talents and abilities. He makes each person unique—one person has this skill, and another person has that skill. People who become doctors have the talents and abilities to do what doctors do.

But people aren't born being doctors. They have to get a lot of training. They have to go to school for a long time and study hard. They have to learn from other doctors who have a lot of experience. Only after they have done all that are they "so smart." They know a lot because they've learned a lot.

KEY VERSE: *Bezalel, Oholiab, and the other craftsmen whom the Lord has gifted with wisdom, skill, and intelligence will construct and furnish the Tabernacle, just as the Lord has commanded. (Exodus 36:1)*

RELATED VERSES: *Exodus 35:31-36; Proverbs 2:6; 17:24; 24:3-4*

RELATED QUESTIONS: *What if the doctors give a person the wrong medicine? Why do people buy medications when they don't need them?*

Q: HOW DOES MEDICINE MAKE SOMEONE BETTER?

191

A: Medicine helps your body heal itself. Some medicines do this by killing germs; antibiotics work that way. Some medicines help the body do what it does even better. Some medicines stop the body from doing what it should not do; some asthma medicines work that way. Doctors often know what medicines to give for each sickness. The purpose of medicine is to help your body do the healing work.

The one thing medicine cannot do is heal your attitude. You can be cured of an illness but remain angry, selfish, and bitter. Or you may not be cured physically but still be thankful, peaceful, and trusting of God. It is important to place your hope and trust in God, no matter how sick you may be. That is what Job did.

In the end, it is God who heals people. God gives us our bodies and gives us the substances that make medicines work.

KEY VERSE: *Then Isaiah said to Hezekiah's servants, "Make an ointment from figs and spread it over the boil." They did this, and Hezekiah recovered! (2 Kings 20:7)*

RELATED VERSES: *Job 2:1-10; Psalm 103:2-3; Proverbs 18:14*

RELATED QUESTIONS: *How do you make medications? How does medicine work? How do "puffers" prevent asthma? How do glasses work?*

Q: WHO INVENTED VEGETABLES?

192

A: God created vegetables—they were his idea. Our bodies need certain kinds of food, just as a car needs a certain kind of fuel. You wouldn't put hamburgers into a gas tank, would you? God gave us vegetables as good food for us because that's one kind of fuel our bodies need.

In fact, vegetables have several very important jobs. First, they provide vitamins and minerals that help us grow and become strong and healthy. Without these vitamins and minerals, our body would not work right. Vegetables also give us fiber, which is the part of plant cells that your body cannot digest. Fiber carries all the other foods through your digestive system. That may sound unimportant, but without fiber, all the other food you eat would get stuck in your digestive tract.

God gave us fruits and vegetables to eat so that our bodies would work properly.

KEY VERSE: *"Test us for ten days on a diet of vegetables and water," Daniel said. (Daniel 1:12)*

RELATED VERSES: *Genesis 1:29; Psalm 104:24*

RELATED QUESTIONS: *Why do parents make you eat tomatoes and onions when you don't want to eat them? How are vegetables good for us? Why are vegetables green?*

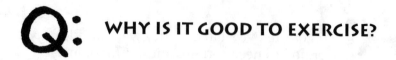

Q: WHY IS IT GOOD TO EXERCISE?

193

A: Your body needs exercise, just as it needs food, air, and water. Muscles need to be stretched and strengthened. The lungs need to breathe fresh, clean air. Joints need to be moved around. Blood needs to get moving. Exercise is a way of taking care of your body. Exercise also helps people lose weight by using the food, building muscle, and burning fat.

Some people today don't get enough exercise—they sit around watching TV, playing video games, or surfing the Internet for a long time. Sitting around all the time is not good for a person's health. You need to get out and use your body. Good exercise comes from working around the house, working in the yard, riding bikes, running, walking, and playing sports.

God gave us wonderful bodies, and he wants us to take care of them. And we all need exercise to do that properly.

KEY VERSE: *Physical exercise has some value, but spiritual exercise is much more important, for it promises a reward in both this life and the next. (1 Timothy 4:8)*

RELATED VERSES: *1 Corinthians 6:19-20; 1 Timothy 5:23*

RELATED QUESTIONS: *How does exercise help lose weight? How does exercising make you lose weight? How come people make machines that make you lose weight?*

Q: WHY DO PEOPLE SMOKE?

194

A: People smoke because they are addicted to the nicotine in the cigarettes. Nicotine is a chemical in tobacco. Once you start putting nicotine into your body, your body starts to crave it. You start to feel like you *need* it. Smoking gives your body the nicotine it craves, and this makes it hard to stop.

People also get addicted to the experience. That is, they get used to having a cigarette at certain times of the day. It becomes a habit.

Most people who smoke started when they were very young. They may have started because they thought that smoking would make them look cool or tough or because they liked the taste. Maybe someone they knew talked them into it. After a while, however, they got tired of smoking—it's not cool anymore. But they have become addicted to the nicotine and find it almost impossible to stop.

It is important for us to take good care of our body. Smoking damages many parts of our body. God didn't make our lungs to breathe in smoke.

Try not to be too hard on people who smoke. Quitting is very difficult.

KEY VERSES: *I don't understand myself at all, for I really want to do what is right, but I don't do it. Instead, I do the very thing I hate. I know perfectly well that what I am doing is wrong, and my bad conscience shows that I agree that the law is good. But I can't help myself, because it is sin inside me that makes me do these evil things. (Romans 7:15-17)*

RELATED VERSES: *Matthew 7:1-6; 1 Corinthians 6:19-20; Galatians 5:22-24*

RELATED QUESTIONS: *Why is smoking bad for you? Does smoking make your lungs gross?*

Q: WHAT DOES CLONING MEAN?

195

A: Cloning means making an exact copy of a living thing's DNA, or genetic code. It involves taking the genetic code of a plant or animal and making another plant or animal from that code. Cloning bypasses the usual means of reproduction from a male and female. It's like making a photocopy of a living plant or animal, or building two houses with the same measurements.

Cloning does *not* mean making an exact copy of a person. Cloning copies only the *body,* not the soul, the spirit, or the experiences that also make a person who he or she is. Even if someone could make an exact physical copy of your eyes, knees, and brain, the clone would still be different from you. Your personality, experiences, desires, dreams, choices, and relationship with God would all be different from the clone's. It is all of these things together that make you one of a kind.

No one could ever be exactly like you. Isn't that great?

KEY VERSE: *You made all the delicate, inner parts of my body and knit me together in my mother's womb. (Psalm 139:13)*

RELATED VERSES: *Psalm 139:13-16*

RELATED QUESTIONS: *Is cloning going to happen to all animals? How do you clone someone? Why do people argue over medical ethics? What are medical ethics? Can scientists create life in a test tube? Is the life they create in a test tube like a blob or virus?*

196

A: People die because sin came into the world when Adam and Eve sinned. In fact, everyone dies eventually. Some people die when they're young, some die when they're old, and some die when they're in the prime of life. But no matter how long a person lives, his or her life sooner or later comes to an end.

God can heal people and stop them from dying, and sometimes he does. But even a person who has been healed through a miracle from God will die someday.

But God's people know that death is not the end of the story. This life is *not* all there is. People who know God will go to live with him in heaven after they die. So it is very important for us to be ready to meet him when we die.

KEY VERSE: *For we know that when this earthly tent we live in is taken down—when we die and leave these bodies— we will have a home in heaven, an eternal body made for us by God himself and not by human hands. (2 Corinthians 5:1)*

RELATED VERSES: *Romans 8:38-39; 1 Corinthians 15:35-58; 2 Corinthians 5:1-8; Revelation 21:4*

RELATED QUESTION: *Why do children die?*

OUTER
SPACE

Q: WHY IS THERE A UNIVERSE?

197

A: *Universe* is another word for the creation— everything that God created. God created it all. He created every star, every galaxy, every black hole, every atom. And God created everything very good. We don't know why God created everything in the universe, but we do know that he had a good reason.

We also know that God designed the universe for us to live in. The Bible says that God placed the stars and the moon in the night sky to give us light during the night, and the sun to give us light during the day. God had us in mind when he created these things; he gave them their design so that we could live on this earth. They are a sign of God's care and love for us.

The Bible also says that the creation is evidence of God's existence (see Romans 1:20). When people look around and see the earth and all the stars, they know that these things came from God.

KEY VERSE: *By faith we understand that the entire universe was formed at God's command, that what we now see did not come from anything that can be seen. (Hebrews 11:3)*

RELATED VERSES: *Genesis 1:16-18; John 1:3; Romans 1:20; Colossians 1:16-17*

RELATED QUESTIONS: *Why does the world spin around? How fast does the sun travel? How far is Pluto from the sun? Why is there a ring around Saturn? How many moons are there in space? Why is our galaxy called the Milky Way?*

NOTE TO PARENTS: *Creation tells us something about God's power and nature. You can look out at the night sky with your children and talk about what the stars tell us about God.*

Q: IS OUTER SPACE HOT OR COLD?

198

A: Most of outer space is very cold; only the stars and the space right around them are hot. God created the universe with over a billion billion stars. The stars put out a lot of heat, but there is a lot more space than stars. So anything not close to a star has almost no heat at all. The heat produced by the Sun, the star that's closest to Earth, produces just the right amount of light and heat for us to live on our planet. The air on Earth keeps the heat in. God created the earth with just the right climate so that human beings, his special creations, could live here. Earth is our home.

KEY VERSES: *When I look at the night sky and see the work of your fingers—the moon and the stars you have set in place—what are mortals that you should think of us, mere humans that you should care for us? (Psalm 8:3-4)*

RELATED VERSES: *Psalm 33:6; Proverbs 3:19-20; Colossians 1:15-17*

RELATED QUESTIONS: *How come it's cold in space? Why did God make so many different planets?*

Q: WHY DO PEOPLE WANT TO FLY TO OTHER PLANETS?

COLLECTING FOR NASA'S SPACE STATION

199

A: Some people want to travel to other planets because they want to know how the universe began. Even those who believe that God created every-thing are curious about how he did it. The stars, the planets, and all the universe are marvelous displays of God's handiwork.

Other people are simply curious. They want to travel to other planets to see them up close, to see what it would be like to go there, and to learn all they can. It would certainly be an adventure!

KEY VERSE: *It is God's privilege to conceal things and the king's privilege to discover them. (Proverbs 25:2)*

RELATED VERSES: *Psalm 19:1-6; Proverbs 25:3*

RELATED QUESTIONS: *How come astronauts went up to outer space to find planets? Why do people want to build settlements on other planets? How would people get oxygen if they lived on Mars? How would people get supplies up to Mars? Why do some people think there is life on Mars? How would little germs or worms survive on Mars? How would life on Mars live without oxygen?*

Q: IF THERE'S INTELLIGENT LIFE ON OTHER PLANETS, DO THEY HAVE TEACHERS?

200

A: The universe is so big that we can't even imagine how big it is. The nearest star, Alpha Centauri, is 25 *trillion* miles from our sun, and Alpha Centauri has no planets. It is possible that God created life on other planets, far, far away. But we don't know anything about that because we have no evidence for other living beings on other planets. And even if we could travel at the speed of light, which is over 600 million miles per hour, it would take us over four years just to go to Alpha Centauri. Unless we invent some form of space travel that takes us across the galaxy faster than light, we will probably never know whether God created life on other planets. Only God knows exactly what he created far out in space.

KEY VERSE: *The Lord merely spoke, and the heavens were created. He breathed the word, and all the stars were born. (Psalm 33:6)*

RELATED VERSES: *Proverbs 3:19-20; 25:2-3; Colossians 1:15-17*

RELATED QUESTIONS: *Why do people think there is life on other planets? Are aliens smarter than earth people? Why do people think beings from other planets are smarter than earth people?*

Q: WHY DO PEOPLE THINK THAT BEINGS FROM OTHER PLANETS HAVE VISITED EARTH?

A: Some people believe that beings from other planets have visited earth. Here are some of the reasons they think so:

1. It would be exciting if it were true (wishful thinking).
2. It is one way people explain certain things that used to be hard to explain, such as how the pyramids in Egypt were built.
3. They know there is more to our existence than just ourselves, but they refuse to believe in God, so they look in outer space instead.
4. They want to connect to something that is beyond what they know or experience on earth.

Some people even think that human beings were put on earth by beings from outer space. They do not believe in God or that God created us, and this is the way they explain where we came from.

KEY VERSE: *It should be explained that all the Athenians as well as the foreigners in Athens seemed to spend all their time discussing the latest ideas. (Acts 17:21)*

RELATED VERSES: *Genesis 1:27; Psalm 8:3-8*

RELATED QUESTIONS: *Why do people want to know if there's life on other planets? Is there life on other planets? Are aliens real?*

Q:

WHY DO PEOPLE WANT TO LIVE ON THE MOON IF THEY WOULDN'T BE ABLE TO BREATHE THERE?

A: The main reason for living on the moon would be for learning—studying astronomy and trying to understand the universe better. Some people want to go to the moon to mine it. Some just want to travel and explore.

Few people really want to live on the moon, however, even if the trip were completely safe. It would cost an enormous amount of money to get there. There would be no trees, fresh air, streams, or other things to enjoy. It would also be very difficult to live and to get around. Again, the main reason for going would be to study and do research.

KEY VERSE: *Intelligent people are always open to new ideas. In fact, they look for them. (Proverbs 18:15)*

RELATED VERSES: *Deuteronomy 4:19; Psalm 74:16-17; Proverbs 25:2; Isaiah 45:18; Jeremiah 31:35*

RELATED QUESTIONS: *How can you breathe in outer space? Do they have medicine for people who get hurt up in space? How do they make astronaut suits? How many people have gone to the moon?*

203

A: People who invent marvelous instruments like the Hubble telescope are very talented and intelligent people. God gave them the brains and ability to think of such things. God let them learn and develop the skills to make their inventions. They read, investigated, learned, and studied hard for a long time. The skills and knowledge that people like that use to create such amazing tools come from God, and those people have used them well.

It is a beautiful part of human nature to be able to create and invent things that are useful to us. It is a part of God's image in us. It is a part of God's image in you.

KEY VERSE: *For you made us only a little lower than God, and you crowned us with glory and honor. (Psalm 8:5)*

RELATED VERSES: *Genesis 1:27; Job 38:36; Proverbs 3:13, 19*

RELATED QUESTIONS: *How far can the Hubble telescope see? How do people get the pictures from the Hubble telescope? Why don't they bring the Hubble telescope back down to Earth?*

Q: CAN KIDS BE ASTRONAUTS IF THEY GET TRAINED?

204

A: Kids can't be astronauts because it takes so long to train for it. It takes many years of training and conditioning to withstand the rigors of space flight. Your body has to be in top shape and strong. Even if a young person were chosen to be an astronaut, he or she would be quite a bit older at the end of the training. So you might say that a kid can't be an astronaut, but a kid can train to become an astronaut when he or she is older.

Very few people actually become astronauts, although thousands try. Only the very best get chosen.

KEY VERSES: *Remember that in a race everyone runs, but only one person gets the prize. You also must run in such a way that you will win. All athletes practice strict self-control. They do it to win a prize that will fade away, but we do it for an eternal prize. (1 Corinthians 9:24-25)*

RELATED VERSES: *Luke 2:39-40; 1 Corinthians 13:11; 1 Timothy 4:12*

RELATED QUESTIONS: *I know astronauts have to go through training, but can't kids go to space if they get trained? Why aren't children allowed to be astronauts? What if they were trained?*

NOTE TO PARENTS: *Whenever your children are interested in doing something difficult with their life, try not to discourage them from trying just because it takes a lot of effort. Instead, encourage their vision, pray with them about it, and let them know what they have to do to get there.*

THE
BEGINNING
AND
THE END

Q: WHY DID GOD CREATE THE WORLD?

JASON'S IMAGINATION

IDEAL FOR BILLIONS OF PEOPLE!

LOTS OF WATER!

OXYGEN & MUCH MORE!

PETS WELCOME!

AVAILABLE IMMEDIATELY

205

A: God has not told us exactly why he created the world. We know that God enjoys making things, and that he wanted to be with us. God created people because he wanted to have friends—men and women, boys and girls with whom he could share his love. He created the world for us to live in and enjoy. God loves us. Perhaps that is all the reason he needed.

KEY VERSE: *For the Lord is God, and he created the heavens and earth and put everything in place. He made the world to be lived in, not to be a place of empty chaos. "I am the Lord," he says, "and there is no other." (Isaiah 45:18)*

RELATED VERSES: *Genesis 1:1; Psalm 148:5-6; John 1:1-14; 3:16; Acts 17:27; Colossians 1:15-17*

RELATED QUESTIONS: *How come God created the earth? Why did God rest on the seventh day? What is the big bang theory?*

Q: HOW WAS GOD CREATED?

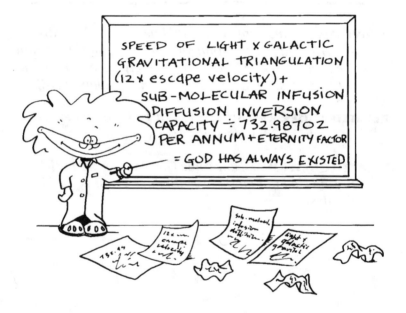

206

A: God was not created; he has always existed. This is impossible for us to understand because everything else we know about has a beginning and an end. But God had no beginning, and he has no end. He always was, and he always will be.

Imagine going on a deep-sea dive and being able to talk to the fish at the bottom of the sea. Imagine trying to explain to the fish what life is like for humans above the surface of the water and on land. The fish would not be able to understand, no matter how hard you tried to explain it. Everything he knows is in the water. *You* can breathe air and walk on the land, but the fish knows nothing about that. So the fish thinks it's silly or impossible.

That is the way it is with God. God created everything we know, including time. Beginnings and endings are limitations of our world, but not of God. That is one of the great things about him—he is so much greater than we are!

KEY VERSES: *In the beginning the Word already existed. He was with God, and he was God. He was in the beginning with God. He created everything there is. Nothing exists that he didn't make. (John 1:1-3)*

RELATED VERSES: *Exodus 3:14; Revelation 1:8; 4:8-11; 5:14*

RELATED QUESTIONS: *How did God get made? Why do people think God has a white beard and is sitting on a throne in heaven?*

Q: WHY DO SOME PEOPLE BELIEVE THAT HUMANS CAME FROM MONKEYS?

207

A: Many people today believe that human beings descended from apelike creatures millions of years ago. In other words, they believe that way, way back in time certain animals changed so that they eventually became human. This is known as the theory of evolution.

There are three main reasons that people believe this: (1) They prefer *not* to believe that God created Adam and Eve and that all people descended from those two people, so they need another explanation. (2) Many scientists tell us that the theory of evolution explains the fossil record. Therefore, it seems reasonable to people. (3) So many *other* people believe the theory of evolution that they assume it must be true.

The Bible teaches, however, that God created human beings at a certain time and that he created them "in his own image" (Genesis 1:27). This means that humans are not just smart animals. Every human being is a special creation of God. The Bible also says that only God was witness to creation.

KEY VERSE: *So God created people in his own image; God patterned them after himself; male and female he created them. (Genesis 1:27)*

RELATED VERSES: *Job 38:1–40:1; Revelation 4:11*

RELATED QUESTIONS: *If we come from monkeys, where did monkeys come from? What is evolution? What's the theory of evolution? How do we know that everything didn't evolve?*

NOTE TO PARENTS: *Evolution is merely a theory—one way of explaining the past. Many textbooks and teachers today present it as fact, but it is not. Explain this to your children so they will be prepared for discussions in school.*

Q: CAN YOU FIGURE OUT HOW OLD THE EARTH IS BY YOURSELF?

208

A: No. Scientists have come up with ways to figure out how old the world is, but no one can know for sure whether these ways are true, and it is impossible to test them because no one can go back in time. There is no book that tells about everything that happened since the creation of the earth. Not even the Bible has an unbroken record of history. Many people think that the earth is billions of years old; others think it is much younger. But no one really knows how old the earth is, and there is no foolproof way to find out.

What we do know is this: God created Adam and Eve and all life on earth many thousands of years ago. It was not an accident or a product of time—it was God's doing.

KEY VERSES: *Where were you when I laid the foundations of the earth? Tell me, if you know so much. Do you know how its dimensions were determined and who did the surveying? What supports its foundations, and who laid its cornerstone as the morning stars sang together and all the angels shouted for joy? (Job 38:4-7)*

RELATED VERSES: *Genesis 1:1-31; Job 38:8-30; John 1:3; Colossians 1:16*

RELATED QUESTIONS: *Does the Bible actually say how old the world is? How old is the world?*

Q: WHY IS THE WORLD GETTING OVERPOPULATED?

209

A: Some people say the world is getting overpopulated, but it is not true. There is plenty of room for everyone. It is true that many *cities* have too many people. In fact, in some places thousands of poor people live in an area that is much too small for them. And in some areas people do not get enough food. But the world itself has enough room for everyone, and it has enough farmland to grow food for everyone too.

Selfishness is a bigger problem than the threat of overpopulation. If people would help each other and always be kind to each other, hunger and overcrowding would not be so much of a problem.

KEY VERSES: *Children are a gift from the Lord; they are a reward from him. Children born to a young man are like sharp arrows in a warrior's hands. How happy is the man whose quiver is full of them! He will not be put to shame when he confronts his accusers at the city gates. (Psalm 127:3-5)*

RELATED VERSES: *Genesis 1:28; Proverbs 11:25; Acts 2:44-45*

RELATED QUESTIONS: *How many people should there be on earth? How come people think the world is overpopulated? Is it all right if you have 4 billion people on earth?*

Q: WHEN IS JESUS COMING BACK TO EARTH?

210

A: When Jesus ascended into heaven, angels promised that he would return, just as he said. But Jesus said that he would return when people least expect it. So no one knows exactly when he is coming back. It could be today; it could be far, far in the future.

That is why Jesus told us to be ready for his return all the time. We should stay close to God and always do what is right.

Although no one knows when Jesus will return, we do know that every day brings his return closer. And when he comes, it will be a wonderful day for those who love him. He will create a new heaven and a new earth where his people will live with him forever. He will put an end to all evil, suffering, pain, and death. And we will get to be with friends and family who love Jesus, all happier than we can possibly imagine now.

KEY VERSES: *However, no one knows the day or hour when these things will happen, not even the angels in heaven or the Son himself. Only the Father knows. And since you don't know when they will happen, stay alert and keep watch. (Mark 13:32-33)*

RELATED VERSES: *1 Corinthians 15:51-58; 1 Thessalonians 4:15–5:11; 2 Thessalonians 1:7-10; 2:1-6*

RELATED QUESTIONS: *Is God really going to come back to earth? How come Jesus didn't say when he was coming back? Why do people think that God will come back? Could Jesus come back right now? Why will nonbelievers be afraid when Jesus comes back? Why isn't God coming back right now?*

Q: HOW IS GOD ALWAYS THERE?

211

A: God can always be with us because he does not have a physical body. God does not have to stay in one place the way we do. We don't know exactly how this works, but that's OK. God is much, much greater and more amazing than we can imagine. Isn't it great to know that God is there . . . and here?

KEY VERSE: *Teach these new disciples to obey all the commands I have given you. And be sure of this: I am with you always, even to the end of the age. (Matthew 28:20)*

RELATED VERSES: *Psalm 46:1; 139:7-12; John 14:16-17*

RELATED QUESTION: *How can God see everything?*

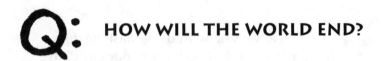

Q: HOW WILL THE WORLD END?

212

A: We don't know exactly *how* the world will end, but we know that it *will* end—the world will not go on forever. This is not bad news; it is part of God's plan. The world will not be destroyed by people or by things getting out of control. It will be God's doing and in God's timing. It will end in a blaze of fire! God will replace this world with a new one.

But it will not happen until Jesus comes back. He will return, just as he promised, to judge all people who have ever lived and to set up his kingdom. He will replace our damaged world with a new, perfect one, where his people will live with him forever. For those who love him, the end of the world will really be a beginning—a wonderful, awesome beginning!

KEY VERSE: *Then I saw a new heaven and a new earth, for the old heaven and the old earth had disappeared. And the sea was also gone. (Revelation 21:1)*

RELATED VERSES: *2 Peter 3:7; Revelation 21:1–22:6*

RELATED QUESTION: *Is the end of the world ever going to happen?*

Q: WHY DOES ETERNITY LAST FOR A LONG, LONG, LONG, LONG TIME?

213

A: It doesn't. It lasts forever, and that's longer than a long time. That's what the word *eternity* means—"infinite or endless time."

It is impossible for people to understand eternity. It's beyond what our brain can imagine, because everything we imagine has limits. But God knows because he has no limits, and he is eternal.

KEY VERSE: *God has made everything beautiful for its own time. He has planted eternity in the human heart, but even so, people cannot see the whole scope of God's work from beginning to end. (Ecclesiastes 3:11)*

RELATED VERSES: *Psalm 119:89-90; Isaiah 26:4; Daniel 4:34; John 3:16; Revelation 7:12*

RELATED QUESTION: *How do I understand eternity?*

Q: IF THE BIBLE SAYS WE'LL LIVE FOR ETERNITY, WHY IS THERE AN END ON EARTH?

214

A: The earth was not made to last forever. Things only last forever if God wants them to. God has determined that the world the way it is now will be destroyed and then made new again. God will give us a new heaven and a new earth to replace the old one. The new earth will be perfect in every way, as God intended it to be.

But people *will* last forever. When Jesus returns to make the world new, he will judge every person who has ever lived. Those who have received his forgiveness will be welcomed into his home, to live with him forever. And those who have refused his forgiveness will be cast into the lake of fire. That is why Jesus came, "so that everyone who believes in him will not perish but have eternal life" (see John 3:16).

KEY VERSES: *For all creation is waiting eagerly for that future day when God will reveal who his children really are. Against its will, everything on earth was subjected to God's curse. All creation anticipates the day when it will join God's children in glorious freedom from death and decay. For we know that all creation has been groaning as in the pains of childbirth right up to the present time. (Romans 8:19-22)*

RELATED VERSES: *Matthew 25:46; John 3:16; 2 Peter 3:7; Jude 1:14-15; Revelation 21:1*

RELATED QUESTIONS: *Will we all be adults in heaven? Why is there an end of the world anyway; can't it go on forever? Why do people say that the end of the world is coming? Would anybody be living at the end of the world?*